Knights of the Wehrmacht

KNIGHT'S CROSS HOLDERS OF THE FALLSCHIRMJÄGER

Franz Kurowski

Knights of the Wehrmacht

Knight's Cross Holders of the Fallschirmjäger

FRANZ KUROWSKI

Schiffer Military/Aviation History
Atglen, PA

Translated from the German by David Johnston

Copyright © 1995 by Schiffer Publishing Ltd.
Library of Congress Catalog Number: 94-69827

Printed in the United States of America.
ISBN: 0-88740-749-8

Published by Schiffer Publishing Ltd.
77 Lower Valley Road
Atglen, PA 19310
Please write for a free catalog.
This book may be purchased from the publisher.
Please include $2.95 postage.
Try your bookstore first.

We are interested in hearing from authors with book ideas
on related topics.

FOREWORD

The operations of the German parachute troops (Fallschirmjäger) on all fronts in the Second World War, in parachute actions, glider landings and ground combat, has already been described in numerous publications.

What has so far been missing is a handy supplementary work containing brief profiles of each wearer of the Knight's Cross and higher grades of this decoration.

As the author of military history books I have concerned myself in several works with the former German parachute troops. In the course of these efforts I have been asked several times to write such a supplementary volume.

It was Generaloberst Kurt Student who, during a visit to his home, urged me to create a book naming all the decorated members of the parachute troops and thus create a lasting monument to them.

Other former soldiers of the parachute troops took up this theme. They pointed out that only a few parachute troops were presented in the existing literature and that this did not do justice to the deeds of all the wearers of decorations.

Now the book is complete. It is intended that it should supplement all the existing works on the German parachute troops and by means of numbers, dates and photographs provide information about those men who exceeded themselves and all others in providing a shining example in courage and willingness to sacrifice.

Dortmund, January 1995   Franz Kurowski

HERBERT KARL ABRATIS

Born on March 21, 1918 in Babienten, Sensburg District, East Prussia.
Ultimate rank: Major.
Last service position: Commander of the 27th Parachute Regiment.
German Cross in Gold on March 15, 1943.
Knight's Cross on October 24, 1944 as commander of II Battalion, 1st Parachute Regiment with the rank of Hauptmann.
Killed in action during the night of March 29, 1945 south of Stettin.

Karl Abratis joined the 11th Flak Regiment as a volunteer on March 3, 1936. He became a reserve officer candidate and on March 16, 1939, now a *Leutnant*, was assigned to the 6th Battery, 11th Flak Regiment, Neuhufen as battery officer.

On February 12, 1940 Abratis was attached to the Döberitz Infantry School and on April 21 was transferred to the 7th Air Division. Subsequently he joined the 1st Company, 1st Parachute Regiment, commanded by *Oberleutnant* Schmidt, with which he took part in the action in Gudbrandsal, Norway. Abratis took part in the Crete operation as platoon leader in 1st Company, 1st Parachute Regiment and received the Iron Cross, Second Class there on June 19, 1941.

In Russia Abratis saw action in the Orel combat zone. He led 7th Company, 1st Parachute Regiment and on August 27, 1942 won the Iron Cross, First Class.

In the Italian Theater Abratis, promoted to *Hauptmann* on September 1, 1943, participated in the fighting near Ortona. Following the defensive battles as part of Battle Group Schulz and the 1st Parachute Regiment, on February 7, 1944 he took over the defense of Calvary Mountain. *Hauptmann* Abratis led the 1st Parachute Regiment's II Battalion, initially in an acting capacity and from April 15, 1944 as commanding officer. He and his battalion helped prevent the Allies from breaking through to the Via Casilina. During the night of March 16 he was sent to the city of Cassino, where he and his 7th Company, 1st Parachute Regiment repulsed an attack by New Zealand forces, preventing the fall of the city.

On February 2, 1945 Abratis became commander of the 53rd Parachute Anti-tank Battalion, before taking command of the 9th Parachute Division's 27th Parachute Regiment on February 12. On March 28 he and his unit were engaged in defensive fighting in the breach in the Oder Front south of Stettin-Rosengarten. That night Abratis was killed in action.

HEINZ PAUL ADOLFF

Born on June 29, 1914 in Backnang, Württemberg.
Ultimate rank: Major.
Last service position: Commander of the 1st Parachute Pioneer Battalion.
German Cross in Gold on March 30, 1942.
Knight's Cross on March 26, 1944 as commander of the 1st Parachute Pioneer Battalion, 1st Parachute Division with the rank of Hauptmann.
Killed in action on July 17, 1943 at the Primasole bridge near Raitano, Sicily.

On October 28, 1935 Paul Adolff joined the 17th Motorized Pioneer Battalion's 3rd Company in Würzburg.

After completing the parachutist-rifleman course in Wittstock on July 27, 1940, he became a member of the German parachute troops as platoon leader in 1st Company, 7th Parachute Pioneer Battalion.

Adolff won both Iron Crosses in the campaign against France. He also participated in the Balkan Campaign, the invasion of Crete and the murderous battle in the cold Russian winter of 1941, becoming an *Oberleutnant* on July 2, 1941. Adolff won the German Cross in Gold in the fighting at the Neva, and he returned for another tour of duty in Russia in the autumn of 1942. On January 25, 1943 Adolff was promoted to *Hauptmann* before taking his battalion into action in the southern sector of the Eastern front.

For Adolff and his battalion the Battle of Sicily began on July 13, 1943, when they took off for Rome. From there they were flown via Naples to Catania, where Adolff and his men parachuted into Sicily. With the two companies at his disposal, Adolff was able to prevent the Allies from taking the bridge near Simeto, holding out until the arrival of the 4th Parachute Regiment under *Oberstleutnant* Walther. However, the British 23rd Armored Brigade exerted pressure on the defenders and the bridge had to be abandoned. When the last 88mm Flak, which had knocked out eight enemy tanks, was put out of action, Paul Adolff tried to blow up the bridge. He drove a truck loaded with two aerial bombs onto the bridge in order to detonate them there. Two attempts failed. On July 17 Adolff tried a third time. He was severely wounded in the process and died soon afterward. Paul Adolff was awarded the Knight's Cross posthumously.

GUSTAV ALTMANN

Born on April 13, 1912 in Britz, Eberswalde District.
Ultimate rank: Major.
Last service position: Officer in the Staff of the Commander-in-Chief of the Luftwaffe.
Knight's Cross on May 12, 1940 as an Oberleutnant and commander of "Assault Group Stahl," whose objective was the Veldwezelt Bridge over the Albert canal.
Died on February 20, 1981 in Reinhardshagen, Kassel District.

On April 10, 1931 Altmann entered the Kiel Police School as a police cadet. From there he joined the Wecke State Police Group in 1933 and thus became a member of the General Göring Regiment on October 1, 1935. After becoming a *Leutnant* following an officer selection course Altmann served with various units. Finally, on September 1, 1939, he joined 1st Parachute Regiment's 1st Company in Stendal. On April 1, 1939 Altmann was promoted to *Oberleutnant* and was seconded to the "Friedrichshafen Trials Battalion," which was the cover name for the Koch Assault Battalion.

Within the Koch Assault Battalion Altmann led Assault Group "Stahl." Its mission was to parachute into Belgium, take the Veldwezelt Bridge over the Albert Canal and hold it until army units arrived. The plan was a success. In spite of fierce attacks and heavy artillery fire, the bridge was held until the arrival of the 33rd Rifle Regiment.

On May 12, 1940 Gustav Altmann received both Iron Crosses and the Knight's Cross. On May 16 he was promoted to *Hauptmann* for bravery in the face of the enemy. Altmann was captured by the British on May 22, 1941 during the airborne invasion of Crete and did not return home until after the war. His actions in Crete were acknowledged in a Wehrmacht communique of June 9, 1941, along with those of *Major* Koch, *Oberleutnant* Genz and the other commanders on the island.

On September 24, 1942, while a prisoner of war, Altmann learned of his promotion to *Major*.

HELMUT ARPKE

Born on March 3, 1917 in Graudenz, West Prussia.
Ultimate rank: Oberleutnant.
Last service position: Commander of 3rd Company, 1st Parachute Assault Regiment.
Knight's Cross on January 16, 1942 as commander of 3rd Company, 1st Parachute Regiment with the rank of Leutnant.
Killed in action on January 16, 1942.

Helmut Arpke joined the Luftwaffe on October 1, 1935 and after completing an NCO course reported to I Battalion, 1st Parachute Regiment on September 1, 1939. Arpke participated in the campaign in Poland. Promoted to *Feldwebel* on May 1, 1940, on May 12 he won both Iron Crosses as a platoon leader in *Oberleutnant* Altmann's company for actions near Veldwezelt. Arpke and his pioneer squad cut the fuses leading to the explosive charges on the bridge under heavy enemy fire and put out of action a 15-man machine-gun bunker on the west bank of the canal. Afterward he and his men captured all the barricades on and in front of the bridge.

On November 1, 1940 Arpke was named reserve officer candidate. He became an *Oberfeldwebel* on February 15, 1941 and a *Leutnant* on June 17 of the same year.

Arpke successfully completed the 6th War Officers Candidate Course, which lasted from December 2, 1940 to February 22, 1941, at the 1st Luftwaffe Officer Candidate School.

On Crete Arpke fought within the battalion, proving an example to his men. In the late autumn of 1941 he went to Russia with the 1st Parachute Regiment.

In the bitter fighting at the Neva and subsequently as commander of 3rd Company, 1st Parachute Regiment at Yakolevka and Zhaikovka, Arpke was a steadying influence on his men, the man who always knew a way out. He was fatally wounded in battle on January 16, 1942; Arpke had received the Knight's Cross the same day. On April 1, 1942 Helmut Arpke was posthumously promoted to *Oberleutnant* for bravery in the face of the enemy.

JOSEF BARMETLER

Born on March 11, 1904 in Kempten, Allgäu
Ultimate rank: Major.
Last service position: Commander of II Battalion, 6th Parachute Regiment.
Knight's Cross on July 9, 1941 as commander of 7th Company, Parachute Assault Regiment with the rank of Oberleutnant.
Died on February 20, 1945 as a result of injuries sustained while parachuting into Crete.

Josef Barmetler joined the 19th (Bavarian) Infantry Regiment on April 2, 1924. He had signed up for a period of twelve years. After various postings from the infantry to the mountain troops, he served as a *Reserve Leutnant* and *Oberleutnant* (January 1, 1940) in Germany's defensive line on its western border, the Westwall.

On August 1, 1940 he was transferred to the Luftwaffe at his own request and a month later became commander of the Parachute Assault Regiment's 7th Company.

Barmetler was seriously wounded in Crete on May 25. He had performed well there in the battle for Hill 107 and the elimination of the anti-aircraft guns on the hill, as well as in providing effective support to the mountain infantry on May 25. Barmetler was wounded during the decisive assault on the hill held by the New Zealanders. He was recommended for the Knight's Cross by his battalion commander, *Major* Stentzler, and *Oberst* Utz, commander of the 100th Mountain Infantry Regiment. As a result of his wounds Barmetler was only able to serve at home.

He was promoted to *Hauptmann* on July 25, 1941 and *Major* on June 1, 1944.

The consequences of his wounds were such that Barmetler was hospitalized at the end of 1944. He died in hospital on February 20, 1945.

KARL HEINZ BECKER

Born on January 2, 1914 in Schwedt an der Oder.
Ultimate rank: Oberst.
Last service position: Assigned to command the 3rd Parachute Division.
German Cross in Gold on June 19, 1944.
Knight's Cross on July 9, 1941 as commander of 11th Company, 1st Parachute Regiment with the rank of Oberleutnant.
Oak Leaves (780th recipient) as commander of the 5th Parachute Regiment with the rank of Oberstleutnant.

Becker joined the "General Göring State Police Group" on October 10, 1934. He attended various training courses, advancing from *Fahnenjunker* through *Fähnrich* to *Oberfähnrich* before being promoted to *Leutnant* on August 2, 1936. On February 16, 1937 he became a platoon leader in the General Göring Regiment's 8th (Machine-gun) Company and three months later acting commander of 5th Company, General Göring Regiment.

After attending the 2nd Luftwaffe Officer Candidate School, Becker was assigned to various postings until October 21, 1938, when he was transferred to the General Göring Regiment's airborne (glider) battalion. On January 1, 1939 he became company officer in III Battalion, 1st Parachute Regiment, which was to become his permanent home. His commanding officer was *Hauptmann* Karl-Lothar Schulz. Becker was promoted to *Oberleutnant* on June 1, 1939 and on April 1, 1940 took over the 1st Parachute Regiment's 11th Company. Together with Karl-Lothar Schulz he took part in the operation against Rotteram's airport. Becker distinguished himself in this action and was awarded the Iron Cross, First Class.

Becker participated in the airborne invasion of Crete, taking part in the capture of Heraklion. In the autumn and winter of 1941 he and his company were present during the bloody fighting at the Neva.

On July 1, 1942 Becker became regimental adjutant of the 1st Parachute Regiment. Effective December 28, 1942 he commanded III Battalion, 1st Parachute Regiment and undertook one of the last attempts to relieve the garrison of the fortress of Velikiye Luki under *Oberstleutnant* von Sass.

Becker was wounded on the Eastern Front on January 16, 1943. On May 24, 1943 he was promoted to *Hauptmann* and after recovering from his wounds was posted to the 3rd Parachute Division, assuming command of that unit's 5th Regiment. Becker and his adjutant were named in the Wehrmacht communique on July 29, 1944 during the fighting for St. Lô. Becker and his unit saw action during the Ardennes offensive and he subsequently led the unit back through the Westwall in the final weeks of the war.

ERICH BEINE

Born on June 26, 1914 in Dörentrup, Lemgo District.
Ultimate rank: Major.
Last service position: Commander of I Battalion, 12th Parachute Regiment (Assault Regiment).
Knight's Cross on November 18, 1944 as commander of III Battalion, 12th Parachute Regiment (Assault Regiment) with the rank of Hauptmann.
Wound Badge in Gold on April 19, 1945.

Erich Beine joined the Luftwaffe on April 15, 1936, passing through the various signals schools and taking part in the NCO candidate course at Halle Signals School. On May 15, 1939 he joined 7th Company, Luftgau Signals Regiment 1 in Kraussen. On July 27, 1940 he was transferred to the parachute troops.

Beine was promoted to *Oberfeldwebel* on October 1, 1940 and on November 1 was named an officer candidate. On March 1, 1941 he joined I Battalion, 1st Parachute Assault Regiment and was promoted to *Leutnant*. Beine took part in the airborne invasion of Crete with this regiment.

In the period that followed he served as platoon leader in I Battalion, 1st Parachute Assault Regiment. Beine fought in Russia in the northern sector near Vyborgskaya and Zhaikovka, where he won the Iron Cross, First Class. The decoration was presented to him on February 25, 1942.

On February 15, 1942 Beine assumed command of 5th Company, 12th Parachute Assault Regiment, part of the 4th Parachute Division. The next day he was promoted to *Hauptmann*. With this unit Beine fought in Italy, where on March 19, 1944 he distinguished himself in eliminating an enemy penetration in the area of II Battalion, 12th Parachute Assault Regiment. As commander of III Battalion, 12th Assault Regiment, Beine led a successful counterattack on July 10, 1944. *General der Flieger* Schlemm praised this action in an order of the day.

The fighting in the Florence area and in the Appenine position once again saw Beine successfully repel heavy enemy attacks. In recognition of this he was awarded the Knight's Cross. Beine fought to the last day in Italy and was awarded the Wound Badge in Gold on April 19, 1945. On May 3, 1945 he became a prisoner of war and was released on April 16, 1946.

KARL BERGER

Born on October 31, 1919 in Kolmar, Alsace.
Ultimate rank: Oberleutnant.
Last service position: Adjutant of III Battalion, 15th Parachute Regiment.
Wound Badge in Gold on April 3, 1945.
Knight's Cross on February 7, 1945 as a Leutnant and commander of 10th Company, 15th Parachute Regiment (5th Parachute Division).

On October 5, 1939 Berger left the Reich Labor Service for the Air Replacement Battalion in Neubiberg. There, on December 1, 1940, he joined the parachute troops; Berger underwent parachute-infantry training in Stendal. In spite of his efforts he did not see action in Crete. Not until April 1, 1943, after attending various courses, did he join III Battalion, 4th Parachute Regiment (1st Parachute Division) as a *Feldwebel* and platoon leader. Berger saw action in Russia and won the Iron Cross, Second Class.

Along with the rest of his regiment, which was commanded by *Oberstleutnant* Walther, Berger saw action in Sicily. He fought successfully on the Italian mainland, as evidenced by the awarding of the Iron Cross, First Class on April 13, 1944. As a platoon leader and company commander, and finally as adjutant of III Battalion, 15th Parachute Regiment, Berger fought in Italy and subsequently in Normandy. On July 6, 1944 he took part in an action in which the regiment captured Hill 122 at the northern edge of the Foré de Moncastre. Berger and his battalion fought their way into the forest.

The nocturnal battle of July 11 demanded the utmost of the German forces. *Leutnant* Berger distinguished himself in this action. The entire 15th Parachute Regiment was named in the Wehrmacht communique of July 29, 1944.

In the subsequent fighting Karl Berger succeeded in destroying two enemy tanks from close range. He received the Wound Badge in Gold, the Luftwaffe's Ground Combat Badge and the Close Combat Clasp in Silver. On February 7, 1945 Berger was decorated with the Knight's Cross and on March 1 was promoted to *Oberleutnant*. The end of the war saw him engaged in defensive fighting in the Harz Mountains.

HERBERT CHRISTOPH KARL BEYER

Born on August 4, 1913 in Schlurup near Lübeck.
Ultimate rank: Major.
Last service position: Commander of I Battalion, 4th Parachute Regiment (1st Parachute Division).
Knight's Cross on June 9, 1944 as commander of I Battalion, 4th Parachute Regiment (1st Parachute Division) with the rank of Hauptmann.
Died on September 4, 1966 in Neuss am Rhein.

Karl Beyer joined the Reichsmarine as a seaman on October 1, 1933. He trained on the battleship *Hessen* and served at the naval air bases at List and Hörnum. After taking a submarine course he became a *Feldwebel* on November 1, 1939 and an *Oberfeldwebel* on February 1, 1940. On October 7, 1940 Beyer was named an officer candidate. He subsequently served as a *Leutnant* with the 7th Luftwaffe Propaganda Company (motorized) and on December 11, 1940 was promoted to *Oberleutnant*.

After volunteering for the parachute troops on October 1, 1941, Beyer was transferred to XI Fliegerkorps and was sent to the parachute school in Braunschweig.

After various postings within the parachute troops, on February 1, 1944 Beyer was appointed battalion commander of I Battalion, 4th Parachute Regiment. He had earlier been promoted to *Hauptmann* on July 14, 1943.

On March 16, 1944, during the Battle of Monte Cassino, troops of the 4th Indian Division attacked and captured Hill 193 (Rocca Janule-Castello). The next morning they stormed Hill 435 (the infamous gallows hill). The Indians were now 400 meters deeper in the rear of the "Monte."

On the morning of March 19, 1944 I Battalion, 4th Parachute Regiment under *Hauptmann* Beyer attacked the Rocca Janule. The attack shattered the three battalions of the 5th Indian Brigade assembled there. Beyer had thus prevented them from linking up with the Gurkhas beyond Hill 435 and avoided the subsequent capture of Monte Cassino. In recognition of this feat Herbert Beyer was awarded the Knight's Cross. On May 8, 1945 Beyer was made a prisoner of war. He was released on August 18, 1945.

ERNST BLAUSTEINER

Born on May 16, 1911 in Vienna, Austria.
Ultimate rank: General Staff Oberst.
Last service position: Chief-of-Staff of II Parachute Corps.
German Cross in Gold on September 5, 1944.
Knight's Cross on October 29, 1944 as Chief-of-Staff II Parachute Corps with the rank of Oberstleutnant.

Ernst Blausteiner joined the Austrian Federal Army on September 16, 1929 and after basic training served in the 1st Motor Transport Company in Vienna. On January 2, 1934 he became a *Leutnant* and from January of the following year was 1st Officer in II Battalion, 3rd Infantry Regiment. On June 3, 1935 Blausteiner was assigned to the 1st Air Regiment in Vienna. He then went to the Reich Air Ministry as an *Oberleutnant*. In 1940 *Hauptmann* Blausteiner took part in the Norwegian Campaign with a reconnaissance unit. He won both Iron Crosses as *Staffelkapitän* of 2./ Aufklärungsgruppe 22.

Blausteiner served on the staff of X Fliegerkorps from June 17, 1941 and advanced to become Ia of the Air Commander North and finally of Luftflotte 5.

Promoted to *Major* on April 1, 1942, Blausteiner was taken into the Luftwaffe General Staff and became Ia of XIII Fliegerkorps, later II Parachute Corps. On February 26, 1944 he became the corps' Chief-of-Staff with the rank of *Oberstleutnant.*

While serving in this capacity Blausteiner was encircled in the Falaise Pocket with II Parachute Corps and the Seventh Army in August 1944.

Generalleutnant Meindl, commanding general of II Parachute Corps, was placed in charge of the breakout. He appointed *Major* Stephani, who was killed in the breakout, and *Oberstleutnant* Blausteiner to lead the two spearheads of the 3rd Parachute Division. Both attack forces succeeded in breaking out of the pocket. This resulted in the Knight's Cross for Blausteiner.

On February 25, 1945 Blausteiner was promoted to *Oberst*. Until the end of the war he continued to serve effectively with *General der Fallschirmtruppen* Meindl.

WOLFGANG LEBRECHT GRAF BLÜCHER

Born on January 31, 1917 in Altengottern, Mühlhausen District, Thuringia.
Ultimate Rank: Reserve Oberleutnant.
Last service position: Platoon leader in 2nd Company, 1st Parachute Regiment.
Knight's Cross on May 21, 1941 as a platoon leader in 2nd Company, 1st Parachute Regiment with the rank of Oberleutnant.
Killed in action on May 21, 1941.

Wolfgang Graf Blücher joined the 14th Cavalry Regiment as a volunteer on October 1, 1934. He participated in three reserve exercises by September 24, 1937 and on April 20, 1938 was promoted to *Leutnant.* He had decided to become an officer on October 12, 1937 and served in the 3rd Cavalry Regiment under *Oberst* Feldt. On February 16, 1939 Blücher was assigned to the 12th Anti-tank Battalion. There he volunteered for the Luftwaffe and requested to be assigned to JG 132 Schlageter. The request was turned down and Blücher remained with the 12th Anti-tank Battalion.

On December 16, 1939 Graf Blücher again applied to join the Luftwaffe. This time he was successful. He was assigned to 3rd Company, 1st Parachute Regiment in Stendal and on April 1, 1941 became a platoon leader in 2nd Company, 1st Parachute Regiment.

On May 10, 1940 Graf Blücher's platoon provided support for his regiment's 3rd Company, which had jumped near Tweede Tool and then become involved in heavy street fighting for possession of Dordrecht. Graf Blücher saw heavy fighting in the Dordrecht area. On May 24 he took a strongly-manned nest of bunkers and on May 24 was awarded the Iron Cross, First Class.

Graf Blücher took part in the Crete operation as a platoon leader in 2nd Company. He and his platoon fought their way to Heraklion airport and captured a hill at the eastern end of the field. Wolfgang Graf Blücher was killed in action on May 21, 1941. Three days later he was awarded the Knight's Cross.

Graf Blücher's two brothers, 19-year-old Lebrecht and 17-year-old Hans-Joachim, died with him on Crete. All were members of an old military family.

RUDOLF BÖHLEIN

Born on January 4, 1917 in Roth, Schwabach District.
Ultimate rank: Hauptmann.
Last service position: Commander of II Battalion, 4th Parachute Regiment.
German Cross in Gold on February 24, 1944.
Knight's Cross on November 30, 1944 as commander of 2nd Company, 4th Parachute Regiment with the rank of Oberleutnant.

Rudolf Böhlein entered the army's NCO school on October 1, 1936, completed his training and was assigned to the 140th Mountain Infantry Regiment. He took part in the Polish Campaign as an *Unteroffizier* in the regiment's 7th Company and won the Iron Cross, Second Class. Böhlein subsequently served in the Westwall and participated in the Western Campaign as a *Feldwebel* and officer candidate in 8th Company, 140th Mountain Infantry Regiment.

On August 1, 1941 Böhlein went to Stendal Parachute School. He completed the parachute infantry course and on March 1, 1942 became a platoon leader in 9th Company, 4th Parachute Regiment. Böhlein had earlier been promoted to *Leutnant* on June 17, 1941. He went on to lead the company's pioneer platoon and saw action in Russia in 1942/43, where he received the Iron Cross, First Class on January 4, 1943.

Böhlein went to Sicily and saw action there from December 10, 1943. In 1943/1944 he fought on the Italian mainland with 2nd Company, 4th Parachute Regiment and was named company commander on June 15, 1944.

Oberleutnant Böhlein distinguished himself in the Battle of Monte Cassino, closing a gap in the German front between monastery hill and the city of Cassino. For this he was awarded the German Cross in Gold. Böhlein led a series of nocturnal offensive patrols in which he attacked enemy forces on the Rocca Janule, interrupted their supply lines and brought back a number of prisoners.

Generalleutnant Heidrich, commander of the 1st Parachute Division, recommended Böhlein for the Knight's Cross, which he received on November 30, 1944. On January 1, 1945 he was promoted to *Hauptmann*. Böhlein and his regiment fought their way back through northern Italy and the partisan bands operating there. On May 2, 1945 he was captured by British forces and was released in the summer of 1946.

RUDOLF BÖHMLER

Born on June 12, 1914 in Weimlimdorf near Stuttgart.
Ultimate rank: Oberst.
Last service position: Commander of the 4th Parachute Regiment and leader of "Battle Group Bosco."
German Cross in Gold on April 3, 1942.
Knight's Cross on March 26, 1944 as commander of I Battalion, 3rd Parachute Regiment with the rank of Major.
Died on November 24, 1968.

Rudolf Böhmler joined the Reichswehr on April 5, 1934 and attended Dresden Officer Candidate School and the Döberitz Infantry School. On April 1, 1936 he became a *Leutnant* and platoon leader in the 55th Infantry Regiment, Würzburg. Böhmler transferred to the Luftwaffe on January 1, 1939.

Following promotion to *Oberleutnant*, Böhmler saw action in the Polish Campaign and was decorated with the Iron Cross, Second Class near Wola-Gulowska. Böhmler served as commander of 8th Company, 1st Parachute Regiment in the battle for Fortress Holland. There he received the Iron Cross, First Class.

Böhmler fought in Crete as commander of 8th Company, 3rd Parachute Regiment. After the initial landings he led Parachute Battalion Böhmler, which reinforced the eastern group of forces near Heraklion. He subsequently commanded II and IV Battalions.

During the winter of 1941 Böhmler and his paratroops fought as infantry in the northern sector of the Eastern Front. There he was decorated with the German Cross in Gold. From autumn 1942 to spring 1943 he fought in the southern sector of the Eastern Front. On July 1, 1943 he was promoted to *Major*. Böhmler now commanded I Battalion, 3rd Parachute Regiment.

In Sicily Böhmler fought under *Oberst* Heilmann. He experienced the toughest fighting of his career as a soldier in the Monte Cassino area, where he and his I Battalion, 3rd Parachute Regiment took over the mountain and the monastery in the second Cassino battle. Both remained in German hands. In the third Cassino battle his battalion defended Calvary Mountain. Böhmler was wounded and put out of action before the battle began. He returned to his regiment after his wounds had healed, and assumed command of the unit on August 20, 1944. On January 10, 1945 he became commander of the 4th Parachute Regiment and led the unit until the end came in northern Italy.

BRUNO OSWALD BRÄUER

Born on February 4, 1893 in Willmannsdorf, Jauer District, Silesia.
Ultimate rank: General der Fallschirmtruppe.
Last service position: Command Reserve of the Luftwaffe Commander-in-Chief.
German Cross in Gold on April 13, 1942.
Knight's Cross on May 24, 1940 as commander of the 1st Parachute Regiment of the 7th Air Division.
Executed under military law together with General Friedrich-Wilhelm Müller in the Schaidari Barracks in Greece on May 20, 1947.

Bruno Bräuer served as a cadet in the Annaburg District, Halle from April 27, 1905. He successfully passed a number of courses. When the First World War began Bräuer was a member of the 7th West Prussian Infantry Regiment No. 155. He won both Iron Crosses and when the war was over was taken into the Reichswehr. On August 7, 1919 he became a *Leutnant.*

On January 1, 1920 Bräuer joined the police. When the Wecke State Police Group was founded on February 25, 1933 he became a member, commanding the unit's 1st Company.

As a *Police Major* – from January 1, 1938 an *Oberstleutnant* – he led the General Göring Regiment's I Battalion. On November 23, 1938 he became commander of the 1st Parachute Regiment and January 1, 1939 saw him promoted to Oberst. In the Polish Campaign Bräuer received the Bars to the Iron Crosses, First and Second Class. In the airborne operation against Fortress Holland he led his regiment from the Dordrecht and Tweede Tool areas. There he received the Knight's Cross for "heroic personal actions in the employment and command of his regiment."

Bräuer led the East Group in the airborne invasion of Crete. There too he demonstrated his leadership qualities.

From February 23, 1943 to May 31, 1944 Bräuer was commander of Fortress Crete, and on March 21, 1945 he took over command of the 9th Parachute Division before being assigned to the Command Reserve of the Luftwaffe Commander-in-Chief on account of illness.

Taken prisoner by the British on May 10, 1945, he was delivered to Greece, where he was sentenced to death even though there was no basis for the sentence.

MANFRED BÜTTNER

Born on February 15, 1921.
Ultimate rank: Fahnenjunker-Oberfeldwebel.
Last service position: Leader of the Signals Platoon of I Battalion, 26th Parachute Regiment.
Knight's Cross on April 29, 1945 as commander of 2nd Company, 26th Parachute Regiment with the rank of Fahnenjunker-Feldwebel.

Manfred Büttner entered the Reich Labor Service on April 1, 1939 at the age of 17. On August 26, 1939 he joined the 100th Pioneer Battalion in Hindenburg, Upper Silesia. Büttner took part in the Polish Campaign with this battalion. In the campaign against France Büttner served as a radioman and radio squad leader in the Lehrgeschwader's 9.(H)-Staffel, and after completing a Radio *Oberfeldwebel* course he joined the parachute troops. Büttner joined the 1st Parachute Regiment as a radio squad leader.

In Russia Büttner served as the leader of the 7th Parachute Regiment's regimental signals platoon. On February 25, 1943, while an *Unteroffizier*, he was awarded the Iron Cross, First Class. On October 20, 1943 he became a *Feldwebel*. He fought in Italy and took part in the parachute operation against the island of Elba.

On April 20, 1944 Büttner was promoted to *Fahnenjunker-Oberfeldwebel*; the same day he was named leader of the Battalion Signals Platoon of Battle Group 300 (Parachute Battalion Schluckebier).

Büttner joined I Battalion, 26th Parachute Regiment as leader of the signals platoon on January 15, 1945. He subsequently became special duties officer and commander of 2nd Company.

In March 1945 Büttner's regiment was engaged in bitter defensive fighting on the lower Oder against the Red Army, which was attempting to take the Oder crossings east of Stettin.

The Soviet 47th Army Corps, which was attacking in the direction of Greifenhagen, was attacked by the battalions of the 9th Parachute Division as they arrived. The enemy were halted south of Altdamm. Manfred Büttner distinguished himself in the bitter fighting near Greifenhagen for possession of Fortress Stettin, leading repeated counterattacks to regain the old main line of resistance. *General* Bräuer recommended him for the Knight's Cross, which he received on April 29, 1945.

GEORG LE COUTRE

Born on September 13, 1921 in Memel.
Ultimate rank: Leutnant.
Last service position: Company commander in Battle Group von Heutz.
German Cross in Gold on June 14, 1944.
Wound Badge in Gold on November 5, 1944.
Knight's Cross on February 7, 1945.

Georg le Coutre joined the 1st Replacement Cavalry Regiment in Angerburg on March 18, 1940. On August 1, 1940 he transferred to the parachute troops and on September 1 became a machine-gunner in 4th Company, 2nd Parachute Regiment. He jumped at the Corinth Canal and saw action in Crete, where he was awarded the Iron Cross, First Class as a *Gefreiter* on June 26, 1941.

On December 31, 1941 he was promoted to *Oberjäger* and on January 1, 1942 was made leader of a heavy machine-gun squad in 4th Company, 4th Parachute Regiment. Le Coutre took part in his regiment's tour of duty in Russia. He attended a course for platoon leaders in the Smolensk area and on April 1, 1943 was detached to the 9th Air Warfare School in Tschenstochau. On June 1, 1943 le Coutre was promoted to *Feldwebel*. Le Coutre joined a platoon leaders course in France in July 1943.

Le Coutre was placed in command of 4th Company, 4th Parachute Regiment on February 1, 1944 and saw action in Italy, where he became a *Leutnant* on April 20. On June 14, 1944 le Coutre was awarded the German Cross in Gold.

Sent to Halberstadt for the formation of the 6th Parachute Regiment, on July 1, 1944 he joined the regiment's 9th Company as company commander. The 6th Parachute Regiment's commander was *Oberstleutnant* von der Heydte. Le Coutre saw action on the Cotentin Peninsula and on September 1 became commander of 10th Company, 6th Parachute Regiment. After several times distinguishing himself at Woendrecht and Hoogerheide, le Coutre went to Bergen op Zoom, where he performed another noteworthy feat on October 29. After taking part in the last parachute action in the Ardennes Offensive, he was recommended for the Knight's Cross by the commander of the First Parachute Army's weapons school, *Major* von Huetz. Headquarters, First Parachute Army confirmed the awarding of the decoration.

Leutnant le Coutre was captured on February 16, 1945. He was released from captivity on October 20, 1946.

EGON DELICA

Born on January 4, 1915 in Stettin, Pomerania.
Ultimate rank: Hauptmann.
Last service position: Commander of II Battalion, 19th Parachute Regiment.
German Cross in Gold on December 26, 1943.
Knight's Cross on May 12, 1940 as deputy commander of "Assault Group Granite"/Parachute Assault Battalion Koch with the rank of Leutnant.

Egon Delica joined the 2nd Artillery Regiment in Stettin-Altdamm as a gunner on April 1, 1933. From there he moved to the Luftwaffe as an *Unteroffizier* and on June 1 transferred to KG 152 Hindenburg. After taking an observers course in Prenzlau he flew as deputy observer in an He 111 during the Polish Campaign. After attending the officer candidate school in Klotzsche near Dresden, Delica joined II Gruppe of the 1st Kampf-Lehrgeschwader in Schwerin. On December 28, 1939 he was promoted to *Leutnant* and on January 13, 1940 was transferred to Parachute Assault Battalion Koch. There he led the Witzig Pioneer Platoon for a time from mid-March.

At 04.25 hours on May 10, 1940 Delica took off on the mission against the Belgian fort of Eben Emael. Together with *Feldwebel* Niedermeier's squad he took Works 18, destroyed Works 11, repulsed a Belgian counterattack on Works 18 and at 07.00 on May 11 linked up with the first soldiers of the 51st Army Pioneer Battalion under *Feldwebel* Portsteffen.

Delica won the Knight's Cross and on May 16 received a promotion to *Oberleutnant.*

Delica was appointed *Hauptmann* beim Stab with the 5th Parachute Regiment on April 25, 1942 and saw action in Russia. He was wounded and sent to a hospital in Heidelberg. After further training, on December 10, 1942 he became commander of II Gruppe, Glider Geschwader 2, whose area of operations included the Crimea and the Taman Peninsula. Delica was wounded again in April 1943. Following his recovery, on January 1, 1945 he was placed in charge of II Battalion, 19th Parachute Regiment.

Delica was captured in the Reichswald near Kleve on February 12, 1945. He was released on August 27, 1947.

RUDOLF DONTH

Born on February 16, 1930 in Schreiberhau, Hirschberg District, Silesia.
Ultimate rank: Oberleutnant.
Last service position: Commander of 6th Company, 4th Parachute Regiment.
German Cross in Gold on June 14, 1944.
Knight's Cross while a Feldwebel and commander of 6th Company, 4th Parachute Regiment.

After joining the Wehrmacht on October 1, 1939 Donth was sent to the Luftwaffe Training Regiment in Döberitz, passed through several weapons schools and on July 12 began the parachutist-rifleman course in Wittstock. On completion of the course Donth was assigned to the Headquarters Company of the 3rd Parachute Regiment. From there he saw action in the Crete operation with his regiment, winning both Iron Crosses as a *Gefreiter*. Following a brief stint with 2nd Company, Parachute Ski Battalion, he joined 6th Company, 4th Parachute Regiment as a squad leader. Donth was to remain with this regiment for the rest of the war.

Donth distinguished himself in action in Sicily and on the Italian mainland, before he was given several important missions in Italy which resulted in the awarding of the German Cross in Gold on June 14, 1944.

At the end of October 1944 II Battalion, 4th Parachute Regiment was in action southwest of the Savio. Since April 1, 1944 Donth had proved to be the battalion's most effective leader of reconnaissance and offensive patrols.

On September 1, 1944 Donth was appointed commander of 6th Company. Ten enemy tanks attacked the company; the attack was repulsed . A second attack by nine tanks with strong infantry support was also turned back. The third attack was made by 20 tanks and a battalion of infantry. Donth destroyed six tanks from close range, led a counterattack, relieved two squads and freed a number of wounded comrades who had been captured by the enemy.

Donth led a counterattack against a hill east of Bologna. Three officers and 81 soldiers were taken prisoner and enough weapons captured for two companies.

Near Monte Castellero he defeated a British battalion in a night attack. This resulted in the Knight's Cross for Donth. He was taken prisoner on May 2, 1944 and released on April 30, 1946.

REINHARD KARL EGGER

Born on December 11, 1905 in Klagenfurt, Kärnten, Austria.
Ultimate rank: Oberstleutnant.
Last service position: Commander of I Battalion, 4th Parachute Regiment.
German Cross in Gold on April 3, 1944.
Knight's Cross on July 9, 1941 as commander of 10th Company, 1st Parachute Regiment with the rank of Oberleutnant.
Oak Leaves (510th recipient) on June 24, 1944 as commander of the 4th Parachute Regiment with the rank of Oberstleutnant.

Reinhard Egger joined the 11th Alpine Light Infantry Regiment on April 8, 1929 and by September 1937 had worked his way up to the rank of *Wachtmeister.*

Egger became a *Leutnant* on January 1, 1939 after attending the world-famous Theresian Military Academy in Vienna.

On March 14, 1938 Egger was taken into the German Armed Forces where he joined the parachute troops. On completion of the parachutist-rifleman course in Wittstock he joined 10th Company, 1st Parachute Regiment and on October 2, 1940 became company commander. Egger was promoted to *Oberleutnant* on October 25 and led his company in Crete as part of Karl-Lothar Schulz's battalion. The fighting for the city and subsequent patrols saw him in action beside *Oblt.* Becker in offensive and defensive roles. Egger's actions during the eight days of fighting won him the Knight's Cross, following a recommendation by *Major* Schulz. On April 1, 1942 Egger became commander of I Battalion, 4th Parachute Regiment.

This soldier from Austria fought extremely well in Russia and Sicily, and on April 1, 1942 he was promoted to *Major.*

Egger and his I Battalion, 4th Parachute Regiment saw action in Italy in the third battle of Cassino, and after the wounding of *Oberst* Walther he assumed command of the 4th Parachute Regiment, which accepted him completely.

Reinhard Egger played a key role in the fighting withdrawal up the Italian mainland. On July 31, 1944 an intermediate position he was defending was overrun and Egger was captured.

JOHANN ENGELHARDT

Born on December 11, 1916 in Plauen, Vogtland.
Ultimate rank: Major.
Last service position: Commander of II Battalion, 11th Parachute Regiment.
Knight's Cross on February 29, 1944 as commander of 8th Company, 6th Parachute Regiment (Battle Group Gericke) with the rank of Oberleutnant.

Engelhardt entered Air Officer Candidate School 2, Berlin Gatow, as a *Fahnenjunker* on April 1, 1937. On April 1, 1938 he was assigned to the 1st Parachute Regiment and sent to Stendal Parachute School to take the parachutist-rifleman course. On January 1, 1939 he was promoted to *Leutnant.*

Assigned to the Friedrichshafen Test Battalion (Assault Battalion Koch), he took part in the operation against Fortress Holland and on May 17, 1940 received the Iron Cross, First Class.

On September 1, 1940 Engelhardt took over a platoon in 13th Company, 1st Glider Assault Regiment. On February 15, 1942 he became adjutant of IV Battalion, 1st Parachute Assault Regiment. Engelhardt was promoted to *Oberleutnant* on July 1, 1943 before assuming the duties of adjutant of II Battalion, 6th Parachute Regiment.

July 25 saw Engelhardt commander of 8th Company, 6th Parachute Regiment. He and his company took part in the sensational parachute operation against the Italian headquarters on Monte Rotondo carried out by II Battalion under *Major* Gericke.

On January 29, 1944, immediately after the allied landings near Anzio-Nettuno, Engelhardt saw action within the 12th Parachute Regiment, part of the newly-formed 4th Parachute Division. He distinguished himself in several actions with Battle Group Gericke and was recommended for the Knight's Cross by the *Major*. Engelhardt received the decoration on February 29, 1944.

On June 1 Johann Engelhardt received an early promotion to the rank of *Hauptmann* for bravery in the face of the enemy, and on June 7 was named commander of II Battalion, 11th Parachute Regiment. He served with this unit in Italy until the end of the war. Engelhardt was promoted to *Major* on April 20, 1944.

WOLFGANG ERDMANN

Born on November 13, 1898 in Königsberg, Prussia.
Ultimate rank: Generalleutnant.
Last service position: Commander of the 7th Parachute Division.
German Cross in Gold on January 30, 1943.
Knight's Cross on February 8, 1945 while a Generalleutnant and commander of the 7th Parachute Division.
Took his own life on September 5, 1946 while in British custody at Munsterlager.

World War One was in full swing when Wolfgang Erdmann joined the 3rd Foot Artillery Regiment as an officer candidate on January 10, 1916. The young soldier was assigned to the 26th Foot Artillery Regiment, and then as *Leutnant* and adjutant to the 156th Foot Artillery Battalion. Erdmann won both Iron Crosses.

Erdmann remained with the artillery in the Reichswehr and was detailed to study at the Berlin Technical High School, where he completed his training with the title of Graduated Engineer (Dipl.-Ing.).

On October 1, 1936 Erdmann was transferred to the Luftwaffe General Staff and on July 1, 1937 moved over to the Luftwaffe as a *Major.*

While serving in the general staff, Erdmann was promoted to General Staff *Oberstleutnant* on January 1, 1939. From March 1 to September 30, 1939 he commanded II Gruppe of Kampfgeschwader 4 *General Wever.* Erdmann was decorated with the bars to both Iron Crosses.

In 1943 he commanded the 18th Luftwaffe Field Division for four months and on May 1, 1944 was named Chief-of-Staff of the First Parachute Army. On August 20, 1944 he became commander of the Erdmann Division and on September 24, 1944 commander of the 7th Parachute Division, which he led in action in the final months of the war. In Alsace the division fought in the Hagenau Forest and near Sesenheim. On January 14 it was located at the northern edge of the Hagenau Forest. For these successful attacks *Generalleutnant* Erdmann was awarded the Knight's Cross. *Generalleutnant* Erdmann was captured by the British on May 8, 1945.

WERNER EWALD

Born on October 23, 1914 in Manschnow, Lebus District.
Ultimate rank: Major.
Last service position: Commander of II Battalion, 2nd Parachute Regiment (2nd Parachute Division in Brest).
German Cross in Gold on March 29, 1944.
Knight's Cross on September 17, 1944 as commander of II Battalion, 2nd Parachute Regiment with the rank of Major.

Werner Ewald joined the German Armed Forces on April 15, 1936 as an officer candidate. He initially served in signals, with the 1st Signals Regiment in Dresden and Bernau. He was promoted to *Leutnant* on March 1, 1938.

On July 1, 1939 Ewald joined II Battalion, 2nd Parachute Regiment in Stendal as signals officer. He took part in the Polish Campaign, was promoted to *Oberleutnant* on March 1, 1940 and saw action in Fortress Holland.

With the rest of the 2nd Parachute Regiment Ewald flew from Bulgaria to take part in the action at Corinth Canal. He fought successfully there under *Oberst* Sturm.

Ewald also saw action in the assault on the island fortress of Crete, where he won the Iron Cross, First Class on May 29, 1941.

On May 1, 1941 Ewald was placed in charge of 5th Company, 2nd Parachute Regiment and six months later became company commander. He and his unit fought on the Mius and the Volkhov. Briefly placed in command of III Battalion, 2nd Parachute Regiment, on October 1, 1942 he was placed in command of the regiment's II Battalion. Ewald was also promoted to *Hauptmann* on October 1.

Ewald fought in the defensive battles in the southern sector of the Eastern Front under *Oberst* Kroh and was awarded the German Cross in Gold. On August 11 he became commanding officer of his battalion and with it fought in the approaches to and then in the fortress of Brest. Ewald drove back a penetration by US forces into the northwest part of the city and continued to distinguish himself in action until the surrender on September 20, 1944.

On September 17 Ewald was awarded the Knight's Cross. Together with all the other soldiers in the fortress, Ewald, who on the 17th was promoted to *Major* for bravery in the face of the enemy, became a prisoner of war. He was released by the Americans on May 23, 1946.

FERDINAND FOLTIN

Born on November 30, 1916 in Vienna.
Ultimate rank: Major.
Last service position: Ia of the 7th Parachute Division.
Knight's Cross on June 9, 1944 as commander of II Battalion, 3rd Parachute Regiment with the rank of Hauptmann.

Ferdinand Foltin joined the Austrian Federal Army as a one-year volunteer on September 3, 1936. On April 14, 1938 he was taken into the German Armed Forces as an *Oberfähnrich.*

Foltin served initially with the 107th Infantry Regiment's 6th Company in Bad Kreuznach. He subsequently joined to the parachute troops and took part in the 6th parachutist-rifleman course at Parachute School III, Braunschweig. Foltin became an *Oberleutnant* on August 1, 1940 and a week later took over a platoon of the 5th Company, 3rd Parachute Regiment.

Foltin was severely wounded in the Crete operation. His actions were acknowledged on July 1, 1941 with the awarding of both Iron Crosses.

Following an interim staff appointment, on August 21, 1942 he assumed command of 7th Company, 3rd Parachute Regiment, having led the company in an acting capacity since February 24.

After serving as an ordnance officer with the Ia of the 7th Air Division and the 1st Parachute Division, on January 1, 1944 he became commanding officer of II Battalion, 3rd Parachute Regiment. While in this position Foltin was promoted to *Major* on June 1, 1944.

During the second battle of Cassino Foltin commanded a battle group in Cassino city. On March 15, 1944 the unit's 7th Company was surrounded and wiped out. On the second day of fighting ten enemy tanks were destroyed and two Shermans knocked out by the one available assault gun. On the fifth day of the second battle of Cassino strong enemy armored forces attacked; *Hauptmann* Foltin played a decisive part in the holding of the exposed position. This act won him the Knight's Cross.

After completing general staff training Foltin was assigned to Headquarters, First Parachute Army. On September 1, 1944 he became Ia of the 7th Parachute Division.

Foltin was held as a POW by the British from May 8 to October 20, 1945.

HERBERT FRIES

Born on March 1, 1925 in Waldmühlen, Westerwald District.
Ultimate rank: Leutnant.
Last service position: Commander of a Jagdpanzer IV.
Knight's Cross on September 5, 1944 as vehicle commander and gunner of the tank destroyer "Schlafmütze" of 2nd Company, 1st Parachute Anti-tank Battalion, with the rank of Gefreiter.

Herbert Fries volunteered for the parachute troops on March 10, 1943 after three months service in the Reich Labor Service and on June 25, 1943 arrived in Gardelegen. From there he was sent to Salzwedel for training on anti-tank guns. Fries received further training, including live firing, at Angouleme and Avignon in southern France.

On February 3, 1944 Fries moved with the 2nd Company of the 1st Parachute Anti-tank Battalion to Piedimonte near Cassino. There he took command of a Jagdpanzer IV – his vehicle was equipped with the so-called "Panther cupola" – and saw action with his unit in the third battle of Cassino from the 11th to the 18th of May. After the battle was over twenty paratroops and three tank-destroyers held the village of Piedimonte north of the Via Casilina, preventing a rapid advance by the enemy and the possible encirclement of the 1st Parachute Division.

While the tank destroyer commanded by Schmittsberger was posted southeast of the village, Fries and his vehicle were stationed west of Piedimonte. Farther to the west was Markl's tank destroyer, covering the intersection of the road from Pontecorvo to Aquino and the Via Casilina.

On May 21 the enemy attacked with tanks. Fries knocked out seven Sherman tanks that day and prevented an enemy breakthrough. The second attempt on May 22 again saw the enemy attack with strong armored groups. This time Fries destroyed six enemy tanks and on the next day knocked out another seven Shermans.

Fries was named in the Wehrmacht communique of July 25, 1944 and on September 5 was awarded the Knight's Cross. On October 1, 1944 he was promoted to *Oberjäger* and on April 20, 1945 to *Leutnant*.

Fries was held as prisoner of war in Chieti and Modena from May 10, 1945 until July 24, 1947.

ERNST FRÖMMING

Born on February 4, 1911 in Rotenburg an der Wümme, Stade District.
Ultimate rank: Major.
Last service position: Commander of the 1st Parachute Pioneer Battalion.
German Cross in Gold on June 14, 1944.
Knight's Cross on November 18, 1944 as commander of the 1st Parachute Pioneer Battalion, 1st Parachute Division with the rank of Major.
Died on August 18, 1959 in Rotenburg an der Wümme.

Ernst Frömming joined the Reichswehr on May 1, 1930. After completing basic training he was assigned to the 6th Pioneer Battalion in Minden. From there he was transferred to 1st Company, 19th Pioneer Battalion in Holzminden as a *Gefreiter.*

Frömming served in various pioneer units until May 10, 1940. On April 1, 1941 he was transferred to the 7th Parachute Pioneer Battalion. During this unit's tour of duty in the northern sector of the Eastern Front he won the Iron Cross, First Class.

Together with the rest of his unit Frömming took part in the airborne invasion of Crete. On December 1, 1941 he was promoted to *Oberleutnant.* He advanced to leader of 13th Company (Pioneer), 1st Parachute Training Regiment and on October 8, 1942 was made company commander.

Deployed in the central sector of the Eastern Front near Smolensk, during the night of March 26, 1943 he led an attack which recaptured a strongpoint near Massejnik.

In Sicily Frömming led the 2nd Company of the 1st Parachute Pioneer Battalion, which was employed as a rearguard. Roads and bridges were blown up. In total Frömming and his men destroyed 146 river crossings and laid more than 5,000 mines, stopping the pursuing enemy and enabling German forces to escape across the Strait of Messina.

Frömming and his battalion played an equally significant role in the defensive battle of Cassino.

For these decisive accomplishments and the construction of the Savio Bridge, which enabled the 1st Parachute Division's heavy weapons to cross the river, Frömming was awarded the Knight's Cross.

Frömming was taken prisoner on May 2, 1945. He was released five months later.

WILHELM FULDA

Born on May 21, 1909 in Antwerp, Belgium.
Ultimate rank: Hauptmann.
Last service position: Commander of I Gruppe, Jagdgeschwader 400
(equipped with the Me 163 rocket fighter).
Knight's Cross on June 14, 1941 as a Leutnant and glider leader of 3
Staffel, 1st Glider Geschwader and platoon leader in the "Stein" Group.
Died on August 8, 1977 in Hamburg.

Wilhelm Fulda joined the Wehrmacht on November 1, 1935. After completing basic training he took basic pilot training, attended an NCO course and as a reserve officer candidate served as a pilot with the 52nd Pilot Training Regiment in Halberstadt from October 5, 1939.

Fulda completed glider pilot training and joined 17 Staffel, KGr. z.b.V. 5. His first mission as a glider pilot saw him land troops of the Koch Assault Battalion on the Belgian fortress of Eben Emael. Fulda was promoted to *Feldwebel* on May 1, 1940 and received the Iron Cross, First Class on May 13.

Fulda subsequently served as a training director and on January 1, 1941 was promoted to *Leutnant*. He commanded a glider platoon in Luftlandegeschwader 1 and took part in the action at the Corinth Canal.

Fulda's most daring landing was on Crete during the airborne invasion of the island. On June 14, 1941, as a *Leutnant* and glider pilot in 3 Staffel, Luftlandegeschwader 1, he received the Knight's Cross.

As a pilot in the special transport Gruppe and in that unit's 1 Staffel (Go 242), as well as Staffel leader and finally commander of 4 Staffel, Luftlandegeschwader 1, Fulda flew over Russia and the home front.

On November 1, 1943 Wilhelm Fulda joined the German air defense, where he was assigned to JG 301, the "Wild Boar" Geschwader, and then to JG 4. Promoted to *Hauptmann* on January 1, 1944, he became *Kommandeur* of I./JG 302 and on October 31, 1944 was placed in command of II./JG 301.

On November 25, 1944 Fulda became *Kommandeur* of I Gruppe of JG 400. Equipped with Me 163 rocket-powered interceptors, the unit was engaged in point defense.

ROBERT GAST

Born on March 28, 1920 in Kapsweyer, Südliche Weinstrasse District.
Ultimate rank: Leutnant.
Last service position: Commander of 9th Company, 7th Parachute
Regiment in Brest.
Knight's Cross on October 6, 1944 as combat patrol leader in Brest.

Robert Gast was a member of the parachute troops from the time he entered the German Armed Forces on January 10, 1940, initially serving with 7th Company, 2nd Parachute Regiment. On April 1, 1942 he was promoted to *Unteroffizier* and from March 15 to April 21, 1943 participated in a pre-selection course for wartime officer candidates.

Gast saw his first action in Russia in the autumn of 1941 and fought there until early 1943. While in Russia he won the Iron Cross, Second Class on March 17, 1942; the Iron Cross, First Class followed on January 2, 1943.

On April 20, 1943 Gast became a wartime officer candidate at the Luftwaffe's ground warfare school in Mourmelon. He qualified there and on July 1, 1944 was placed in command of 9th Company, 7th Parachute Regiment. Gast was promoted to *Leutnant* on July 24.

The 7th Parachute Regiment transferred to Normandy in July 1944. Gast and his comrades were among the defenders of the Atlantic fortifications. When the Special Purpose Parachute Regiment was formed on August 1, 1944, Gast was one of those assigned to the new unit from the 7th Parachute Regiment. First contact with the enemy came near Dinant. The regiment withdrew through Dinant into the fortress of St. Malo and was forced to surrender there on August 17.

But in Brest the battle went on. The 7th Parachute Regiment fought a defensive battle in the rubble at the eastern end of the city. *Oberst* Pietzonka was decorated with the Oak Leaves. Whether with the Special Purpose Parachute Regiment or the 7th Parachute Regiment, Robert Gast and his men fought magnificently. Gast was recommended for the Knight's Cross on account of his outstanding work in leading offensive patrols, and was awarded the decoration on October 16, 1944. On September 20, 1944 he and his company were made prisoners of war by the Americans.

ALFRED GENZ

Born on March 8, 1916 in Berlin.
Ultimate rank: Major.
Last service position: Commander of the 29th Parachute Regiment.
Knight's Cross on June 14, 1941 as commander of 1st Company, 1st
Parachute Assault Regiment with the rank of Oberleutnant.

Alfred Genz was one of the original members of the German parachute troops, joining the General Göring State Police Group on April 1, 1935 as an officer candidate.

On January 1, 1938 Genz began the parachutist-rifleman course in Stendal. He became a *Leutnant* on March 1, 1938 and a month later platoon leader in 3rd Company, 1st Parachute Regiment. Later he moved to 4th Company. Genz took part in the campaign in Poland as a platoon leader in 3rd Company, 1st Parachute Regiment. Later he returned to Germany to prepare for the airborne invasion of the island fortress of Crete.

The Wehrmacht communique of June 9, 1941 declared: "In the battle for Crete parachute units under the command of *Major* Koch, *Hauptmann* Altmann and *Oberleutnant* Genz distinguished themselves through their daring and bravery."

Alfred Genz was awarded the Knight's Cross for his actions during the invasion of Crete.

On September 1, 1941 Genz was placed in command of I Battalion, 1st Parachute Assault Regiment. On April 15, 1942, six weeks after being promoted to *Hauptmann*, he was appointed *Hauptmann beim Stab* and commander of regimental units of the 5th Parachute Regiment, with which he saw action in Tunisia. Genz subsequently served in Student's special staff group and finally as an ordnance officer with the Commander-in-Chief of Parachute Troops.

Genz was named commanding officer of III Battalion, 12th Parachute Assault Regiment on December 1, 1943 and on January 1, 1945 was charged with formation of the 4th Parachute Replacement Battalion. On April 1, 1945 Genz was simultaneously promoted to *Major* and made commanding officer of the 29th Parachute Regiment. At war's end he was captured by the Soviets in the St.Pölten-Iglau area and was not released until December 1949.

WALTER GERICKE

Born on December 23, 1907 in Bilderlahe, Lower Saxony.
Ultimate rank: Oberst.
Last service position: Leader of Assault Brigade Gericke.
German Cross in Gold on September 15, 1943.
Knight's Cross on June 14, 1941 as commander of IV Battalion, 1st Parachute Regiment with the rank of Hauptmann.
Oak Leaves (585th recipient) on September 17, 1944 while an Oberstleutnant and commander of 11th Company, 4th Parachute Division.
Died in Alsfeld, Hesse.

Following matriculation, on April 3, 1929 Walter Gericke entered the police school in Brandenburg-Havel. After completing an officer training course, on April 1, 1933 he was accepted into the Wecke State Police Group and on September 1, 1937 advanced to become commander of 11th Company, IV Parachute-Rifle Battalion, General Göring Regiment. On April 1, 1938 Gericke was taken into the parachute troops as commander of 4th Company, 1st Parachute Regiment. On April 9, 1940 he led the forces which successfully took possession of the Storstromm Bridge between Falster and Seeland in Denmark.

During the airborne invasion of Holland Gericke led his company in the parachute action against Dordrecht Bridge and won the Iron Cross, First Class there.

In the invasion of Crete Gericke commanded the Glider Assault Regiment's IV (Heavy) Battalion. He pinned down the enemy on the coastal road east of Malemes and on his own initiative launched an attack in the direction of Chania. His unit captured the citadel there. Gericke was awarded the Knight's Cross for his actions.

One of Gericke's most spectacular actions was the jump into the Italian headquarters on Monte Rotondo after the Italians left the Axis alliance. *Major* Gericke captured 15 officers and 2,000 men in this action and received the German Cross in Gold.

With the formation of the 4th Parachute Division *Major* Gericke took over the 11th Parachute Regiment. This unit formed the first blocking front near Anzio-Nettuno. The awarding of the Oak Leaves was in acknowledgement of his success there.

Gericke received a promotion to *Oberst* on January 30, 1945. On April 5 he was ordered to carry out the formation of the 21st Parachute Division. Gericke was made a prisoner of war on May 8, 1945 and was released on November 9, 1946.

ERNST GERMER

Born on December 15, 1917 in Nienburg an der Saale, Bernburg District.
Ultimate rank: Oberleutnant.
Last service position: Infantry Tactics Instructor at I Parachute Corps Leaders School in Boscochiesa-Nuova near Verona.
German Cross in Gold on May 1, 1943.
Knight's Cross on October 29, 1944 as leader of the bicycle platoon of the Headquarters Company, 1st Parachute Regiment with the rank of Fahnenjunker-Feldwebel.

Germer joined the 52nd Pilot Training Regiment in Halberstadt on April 18, 1939 and from there was transferred to 3rd Company, 1st Parachute Regiment. He took the parachutist-rifleman course in Stendal in July-August 1939. Germer saw action in Poland beginning on September 20, 1939.

Ernst Germer served in Norway from April 9-11, in Holland from May 10-20 and subsequently fought in the battle for Narvik. He received the Iron Cross, First Class in Norway on June 24, 1940.

On May 1, 1941 Germer was promoted to *Oberjäger* and fought in Crete with 3rd Company, 1st Parachute Regiment. In the autumn of 1941 he transferred with the 1st Parachute Regiment to the northern sector of the Eastern Front and took part in the dramatic and costly fighting at the Neva.

The second phase of 1st Parachute Regiment's tour of duty in Russia, in the central sector under the command of *Oberstleutnant* (later *Oberst*) Karl Lothar Schulz, saw Germer constantly in action in offensive and reconnaissance patrols and other actions, which often had to be decided in close-quarters fighting. Germer won the German Cross in Gold at this time and on March 1, 1943 was promoted to *Feldwebel.*

Germer saw action in Italy from July 9, 1943 until the end. In the bitter fighting in the Pesaro area, Germer and his bicycle platoon attacked the local port. He and his men destroyed several tanks with Panzerfaust anti-tank weapons and repulsed enemy counterattacks. As a result positions which had been lost by the 1st Parachute Regiment's III Battalion were recovered. For Germer this meant the Knight's Cross. On November 8, 1944 he received the German Cross in Gold. At war's end Germer was captured by the British, who held him as a prisoner of war from May 2, 1945 until 1946.

SIEGFRIED JOSEF GERSTNER

Born on November 16, 1916 in Passau, Lower Bavaria.
Ultimate rank: Major.
Last service position: Commander of II Battalion, 7th Parachute Regiment in Brest.
German Cross in Gold on June 1, 1942.
Knight's Cross on September 13, 1944 as commander of II Battalion, 7th Parachute Regiment in Brest with the rank of Major.

Following the Bavarian tradition, Gerstner joined the mountain infantry on December 4, 1936 and by August 1, 1940 had risen to the rank of Oberleutnant and commanded a company.

On August 31, 1940 Gerstner moved over to the Luftwaffe and on September 1, 1940 became a platoon leader in the 7th Parachute Pioneer Battalion's 1st Company. On April 16, 1941 he assumed command of the battalion's 4th Company.

Gerstner won both Iron Crosses in Poland and Norway, and after promotion to *Oberleutnant* led 4th Company in the bitter fighting in Crete.

On June 1, 1942 Gerstner was awarded the German Cross in Gold. He saw action in Russia in autumn 1941 and the winters of 1942-43 and 1943-44.

Gerstner was wounded on October 28, 1941 in the fighting at the Neva. He was wounded again on January 6, 1943. After recovering from his wounds, and following promotion to *Hauptmann* on February 1, Gerstner was placed in command of the 2nd Parachute Pioneer Battalion. He attended battalion commanders school and on June 19, 1943 was made commanding officer of the battalion.

Hauptmann Gerstner took command of II Battalion, 7th Parachute Regiment on August 15, 1944. With this unit he fought in Brittany near Landerneau. Under his command the unit destroyed the large arched bridge over the Elorne.

Gerstner and his battalion were frequently called upon to carry out demolition work in the battle for Fortress Brest, denying the enemy entrance to the city. *General* Ramcke recommended him for the Knight's Cross.

On September 19, 1944 *Major* Gerstner was taken prisoner by the Americans.

HELMUT GUSTAV GÖRTZ

Born on August 7, 1911 in Schleusenau near Bromberg.
Ultimate rank: Oberleutnant.
Last service position: Commander of 4th Company, 1st Parachute Regiment.
German Cross in Gold on December 5, 1944.
Knight's Cross on May 24, 1940 as leader of 1st Platoon, 3rd Company, 1st Parachute Regiment with the rank of Feldwebel.
Oak Leaves on April 30, 1945 as commander of 4th Company, 1st Parachute Regiment with the rank of Oberleutnant.
Died on May 3, 1979 in Dinslaken.

Görtz entered Brandenburg-Havel Police School on August 21, 1933 and barely a year later was taken on strength by I Battalion, General Göring State Police Group.

On October 1, 1935 he became a member of the General Göring Regiment's 2nd Company and on August 10, 1936 began the parachutist-rifleman course in Stendal. There he was taken into 1st Company, 1st Parachute Regiment, before finally being transferred to *Hauptmann* Gericke's 3rd Company. Görtz was promoted to *Feldwebel* on November 1, 1939. He took part in the Polish Campaign, won the Iron Cross, Second Class in Norway and the Iron Cross, First Class in Fortress Holland on May 18, 1940. In Holland he was named leader of 1st Platoon. Bitter fighting developed at Dordrecht Station and in the Krispijn district of the city. *Oberleutnant* Freiherr von Brandis, Görtz's company commander, was killed. Görtz and several trusted comrades advanced to the still-open east end of the bridge and halted an attack by the enemy. Görtz held the bridge until the arrival of reinforcements from 2nd and 4th Companies, 1st Parachute Regiment. This action won him the Knight's Cross.

In the winter of 1941 Görtz fought at the Neva River as an *Oberfeldwebel*. In the regiment's second tour of duty in Russia he saw action in the Promklevo area of the Orel bend. Görtz was present when the Russians tried to break through toward Baldusch on March 4, 1943 and he took part in the counterattack toward Aleshenka. On October 26, 1943 he was named a wartime officer candidate.

Görtz's tour of duty in Italy began on July 9, 1943. He took part in the difficult defensive fighting as a platoon leader and on August 8, 1944 was placed in command of 4th Company, 1st Parachute Regiment. Regimental commander *Oberst* Karl Lothar Schulz submitted a recommendation for the German Cross in Gold; Görtz received the decoration on December 5, 1944. It was *Generalmajor* Schulz who recommended Görtz for the Oak Leaves during the 1st Parachute Regiment's final battle. Görtz was awarded the Oak Leaves on April 30, 1945.

FRANZ GRASSMEL

Born on January 8, 1906 in Mochow, Lübben District in the Spreewald.
Ultimate rank: Oberstleutnant.
Last service position: Commander of the 20th Parachute Regiment.
German Cross in Gold on June 15, 1943.
Knight's Cross on April 8, 1944 as commander of III Battalion, 4th
Parachute Regiment with the rank of Major.
Oak Leaves (868th recipient) on May 8, 1945 as commander of the 7th
Parachute Division's 20th Parachute Regiment.
Died on June 30, 1985 in Stade, Lower Saxony.

Franz Grassmel joined the state police at the Brandenburg Police School, Havel on April 5, 1928. After moving to the army, on August 1, 1935 he went to the Anti-tank Battalion in Eisenach. Grassmel served in various anti-tank battalions until June 14, 1940, when he joined the parachute troops in Wittstock as an *Oberleutnant*.

Grassmel participated in the Polish and Western Campaigns. On July 31, 1940 he became commander of 14th (Anti-tank) Company, 1st Parachute Regiment. Grassmel took part in the airborne operation against Crete as commanding officer of this company. Grassmel's four platoons were assigned to the regiment's battalions. One platoon was placed under the command of II Battalion, 2nd Parachute Regiment. Two of Grassmel's anti-tank guns opened the gates to the city of Heraklion. He was awarded the Iron Cross, First Class.

On June 1, 1942, after bitter fighting at the Neva, Grassmel took command of III Battalion, 4th Parachute Regiment. On December 5, 1942, by now promoted to *Hauptmann*, he was made battalion commanding officer. Following his second tour in Russia he received the German Cross in Gold.

Grassmel took off on his second airborne operation as a *Major* (since July 12, 1943) and commander of III Battalion, 4th Parachute Regiment. He and his battalion parachuted into Sicily. On the Italian mainland, Grassmel led the 4th Parachute Regiment for a time in the second battle of Cassino.

On March 19, 1944 the Allies launched Operation "Revenge." Thirty-three tanks attacked Massa Albaneta in an effort to bring about the fall of the abbey. Grassmel's regiment destroyed 29 of the tanks and he received the Knight's Cross.

As commander of Parachute Regiment Grassmel, which was later designated the 20th Parachute Regiment, Grassmel saw action in the Hagenauer Forest as part of the 7th Parachute Division. He and his men fought heroically at Hatten and Rittershofen and in the pitiless fighting withdrawal through the Reichswald into the Edewacht area. On March 1, 1945 Grassmel was promoted to *Oberstleutnant* and on the last day of the war became the 868th German soldier to win the Knight's Cross with Oak Leaves.

KURT GRÖSCHKE

Born on July 17, 1907 in Berlin-Charlottenburg.
Ultimate rank: Oberst.
Last service position: Commander of the 15th Parachute Regiment.
German Cross in Gold on August 11, 1943.
Knight's Cross on June 9, 1944 as commander of III Battalion, 1st Parachute Regiment with the rank of Major.
Oak Leaves (693rd recipient) on January 9, 1945 as commander of the 15th Parachute Regiment, 5th Parachute Division with the rank of Oberst.

Gröschke entered Brandenburg-Havel Police School as a police cadet on October 11, 1927. A year later he joined the Berlin police force and on April 1, 1934 became a member of the General Göring State Police Group. On July 1, 1935 Gröschke became a State Police *Leutnant*. On May 1, 1940, by now an *Oberleutnant,* Gröschke became commander of 2nd Company, 1st Parachute Regiment. He took part in the actions in Poland, Holland and Crete, and on May 22, 1940 was decorated with the Iron Cross, First Class for his efforts in Holland.

Following the Crete operation Gröschke and his battalion fought in the northern sector of the Eastern Front. On February 20, 1942 he became commander of II Battalion, 1st Parachute Regiment.

In the autumn of 1942 Gröschke was involved in anti-partisan operations with the 1st Parachute Regiment under *Oberstleutnant* Schulz, then won the German Cross in Gold in the winter fighting in the Orel area. On January 22, 1944 Gröschke was appointed acting commanding officer of the 1st Parachute Regiment.

Near Casoli on the Sangro River Gröschke stopped an attack by an Indian regiment. He then served as temporary commander of the 1st Parachute Regiment from January 22 to February 11, 1944. On February 8, 1944 his forces prevented the enemy from breaking through to the Cassino-Rome road.

Gröschke was made commanding officer of the 15th Parachute Regiment on July 24, 1944. With this unit he saw action on the invasion front in the West. Gröschke was named in the Wehrmacht communique of July 27, 1944.

In the Ardennes offensive he and his regiment held out against powerful attacks by the American 26th Infantry Division in the area around Harlange until January 10, 1945.

Gröschke was held by the British as a prisoner of war from May 9, 1945 until February 26, 1946.

ANDREAS HAGL

Born on April 21, 1911 in Farchant near Garmisch, Upper Bavaria.
Ultimate rank: Hauptmann.
Last service position: Commander of the rearguard of the 1st Parachute Division.
Knight's Cross on July 9, 1941.
Killed in action in Italy on July 28, 1944.

Andreas Hagl joined the Bavarian Munich Infantry Regiment on October 10, 1931. He underwent NCO training from March to June 1934 and on October 1, 1934 was promoted to *Unteroffizier.*

Hagl voluntarily joined the parachute troops on April 17, 1937. An *Oberfeldwebel* since December 1, 1938, Hagl took part in the fighting in Poland (battle near Wola-Gulowska), where he received the Iron Cross, Second Class.

In the battle for Fortress Holland Hagl won the Iron Cross, First Class, receiving the decoration on July 9, 1940. On November 1, 1940 he became a *Leutnant* and platoon leader in 2nd Company, 3rd Parachute Regiment. Hagl was promoted to *Oberleutnant* on January 16, 1941. He took off with the 3rd Parachute Regiment's I Battalion under *Hauptmann* von der Heydte as part of the airborne invasion of Crete. Hagl and his platoon were dropped in the wrong area and became separated from the main body of the battalion. They fought their way through elements of the New Zealand 10th Division and Greek forces to *Hauptmann* von der Heydte.

Hagl took over the defensive sector on the Cladiso. On May 26 he assumed command of 2nd Company. Although wounded in the right arm he continued to lead the company and played a vital role in I Battalion's success. This won him the Knight's Cross.

Hagl was severely wounded in fighting in the northern sector of the Eastern Front. After recovering from his wounds he was assigned to the officer reserve and on October 15 was transferred to the staff of the 3rd Parachute Regiment as special duties officer. On May 1, 1943 Hagl was promoted to *Hauptmann.*

Hagl saw action in Italy until February 28, 1944, when he was forced to enter hospital again.

As commander of the 1st Parachute Division's rearguard, Hagl was able to ensure an orderly retreat by his division. While serving in this position he was killed in action on July 28, 1944.

REINO HAMER

Born on August 29, 1916 in Rastede, Amerland District.
Ultimate rank: Major.
Last service position: Commander of I Battalion, 7th Parachute Division in Fortress Brest.
German Cross in Gold on July 12, 1944.
Knight's Cross on September 5, 1944 as regimental battle group commander and commanding officer of I Battalion, 6th Parachute Regiment with the rank of Hauptmann.

Reino Hamer joined the 22nd Flak Regiment's II Battalion on December 1, 1936. After training as an aircraft observer in Fassberg-Unterlüss Hamer was assigned to the officer candidate school in Dresden-Klotzsche; from there was sent to I Battalion, 32nd Flak Regiment in Berlin-Heiligensee, where he was promoted to *Oberfähnrich.*

From September 1, 1939 Hamer served as a *Leutnant* with the 32nd Flak Regiment's I Battalion, whose mission was to guard the Reich Air Ministry and Hamburg, and served in Norway as platoon leader and battery commander and later as regimental adjutant.

On March 1, 1941 Hamer became a platoon leader in the Parachute Machine-gun Battalion, Quedlinburg; he attended the parachutist-rifleman course in Braunschweig. Hamer was promoted to *Oberleutnant* on March 1, 1941 and on November 1 became a company commander in the Parachute Machine-gun Battalion. In this capacity he saw action in the Leningrad area at the Neva River.

After training on anti-tank guns, in November 1942 Hamer became commander of the anti-tank company of the 100th Luftwaffe Field Battalion and saw action in the Voroshilovgrad area from December 1942 to February 1943. His actions there won him the Iron Cross, First Class.

Hamer saw action in the fighting withdrawal conducted by the German forces in the southern part of the Eastern Front in 1943-44 as an *Oberleutnant* and commander of 2nd Company, 6th Parachute Regiment and finally as commander of the 6th Parachute Regiment's battle group. On July 12 his efforts were rewarded with the German Cross in Gold. One of his outstanding accomplishments was the elimination of the Soviet bridgehead at Butor, on the Dnestr River east of Kishinev. In this action, which saw three Soviet lines broken, Hamer (promoted to *Hauptmann* since October 1, 1943) distinguished himself through his bravery and leadership qualities. Acting on his own initiative, he and his regimental battle group destroyed the enemy bridgehead.

Hamer was promoted to *Major* and transferred to Fortress Brest as commander of I Battalion, 7th Parachute Regiment. There he led his battalion in a counterattack which eliminated an enemy penetration. This won Hamer the Knight's Cross.

Hamer was captured on September 19, 1944 and remained a prisoner of war until March 20, 1946.

FRIEDRICH HAUBER

Born on March 1, 1916 in Feuerbach, Württemberg.
Ultimate rank: Hauptmann.
Last service position: Commander of II Battalion, 12th Parachute Assault Regiment.
German Cross in Gold on January 1, 1945.
Knight's Cross on September 5, 1944 as commander of II Battalion, 12th Parachute Assault Regiment with the rank of Hauptmann.
Killed in an automobile accident on October 5, 1944.

Friedrich Hauber joined the 9th Flak Regiment in Lippstadt on April 6, 1936. On January 1, 1938 he went to the large military flying school in Fassberg and there was promoted to *Leutnant* on February 24, 1938. On August 1 of that year he was transferred to the 1st Special Purpose Bomber Group, before joining I Battalion, Parachute Assault Regiment on January 1, 1939. Hauber saw action in Holland as a member of this unit. On June 22, 1940 he was promoted to *Oberleutnant*.

Hauber and his regiment fought on the Neva during the winter of 1941-42. On January 5, 1942 he was awarded the Iron Cross, First Class, and on August 24 was promoted to *Hauptmann*. Hauber became commanding officer of II Battalion, 12th Parachute Assault Regiment on December 1, 1943.

In Italy Hauber saw action with Battle Group Gericke in the encirclement of the enemy in the Anzio-Nettuno pocket. At the beginning of September his unit was moved to the "Green Position," in the Viareggio-Pesaro area. There Hauber took part in the bitter fighting against a vastly superior enemy. *Hauptmann* Hauber and *Hauptmann* Beine distinguished themselves in this defensive effort and on September 5 Hauber was awarded the Knight's Cross. He and *Hauptmann* Beine were named in the Wehrmacht communique of September 24.

The 4th Parachute Division fought on in Italy and Hauber saw action in the approaches to Bologna and in the Po Plain. His battalion was encircled by the enemy, but was freed by a mortar battalion commanded by *Major* Knoche. Battalion commander Hauber was sent on leave. On the way to the leave assembly point the driver of his car failed to see a closed railway barrier in the darkness and collided with it. Hauptmann Hauber was killed instantly.

RICHARD HEIDRICH

Born on July 27, 1896 in Lewalde, Saxony.
Ultimate rank: General der Fallschirmtruppe.
Last service position: Commanding General of XI Parachute Corps.
German Cross in Gold on January 1, 1945.
Knight's Cross on June 14, 1941 as commander of the 3rd Parachute Regiment with the rank of Oberst.
Oak Leaves (382nd recipient) on February 5, 1944 as commander of the 1st Parachute Division with the rank of Generalleutnant.
Swords (55th recipient) as commander of the 1st Parachute Division with the rank of Generalleutnant.
Died on December 23, 1947 in Hamburg-Bergedorf.

Richard Heidrich volunteered for military service in the First World War. He became an officer and won the Iron Cross, First Class. After the war he was taken into the Reichswehr, where he served in a number of posts in the infantry.

In 1938 Heidrich commanded the parachute battalion which he had formed as a Major in the infantry. Heidrich and his unit were taken into the Luftwaffe on January 1, 1939. In this way the parachute troops, which were then in the formation process, received a complete II Battalion for the 1st Parachute Regiment. Heidrich was transferred to the staff of the 7th Air Division, but then left the Luftwaffe to lead the 514th Infantry Regiment in the Western Campaign.

In June 1940 *General* Student was able to persuade Heidrich to transfer back to the Luftwaffe. He formed the 3rd Parachute Regiment which he led with great success in Crete.

In November 1942 Heidrich commanded the 1st Parachute Division, which was deployed on the Eastern Front.

The 1st Parachute Division's toughest fighting came after the allied landings on the Italian mainland, particularly in the three battles of Cassino. Elements of the division under Heidrich's command also participated in the fighting at Anzio-Nettuno. Made commanding general of I Parachute Corps, Heidrich oversaw the corps' withdrawal up the entire length of Italy.

Heidrich was captured by the Americans on May 2, 1945 and was later handed over to the British. He died in a hospital in Hamburg-Bergedorf on December 23, 1947.

LUDWIG HEILMANN

Born on August 9, 1903 in Würzburg.
Ultimate rank: Generalmajor.
Last service position: Commander of the 5th Parachute Division.
German Cross in Gold on March 15, 1942.
Knight's Cross on June 14, 1941 as commander of III Battalion, 1st Parachute Regiment with the rank of major.
Oak Leaves (412th recipient) on March 2, 1944 as commander of the 3rd Parachute Regiment with the rank of Oberst.
Swords (67th recipient) on May 15, 1944 as commander of the 3rd Parachute Regiment with the rank of Oberst.
Died on October 26, 1959 in Kempten, Allgäu.

Ludwig Heilmann entered the Reichswehr in early 1921, passing through the hard school of this elite force. In 1933, having served twelve years, Heilmann left the service, but after taking a number of courses he was reactivated on July 1, 1934 as an *Oberleutnant* and commander of 5th Company, 20th Infantry Regiment. In France he won the Iron Cross, First Class with III Battalion, 91st Infantry Regiment.

Heilmann joined the parachute troops on June 18, 1940. After various courses and postings *Major* Heilmann became commander of III Battalion, 1st Parachute Regiment. His battalion was dropped into Crete on May 20, 1941 as part of the first wave. The fighting was bitter and Heilmann's battalion played a part in the German success on the island.

In late autumn 1941 Heilmann and his battalion were sent to Russia, where they fought as infantry. Among the unit's actions was the defense of the blood-soaked Vyborgskaya bridgehead. Heilmann was promoted to *Oberstleutnant* on April 20, 1942. On August 10, 1943 he became commander of IV Battalion, 3rd Parachute Regiment and on November 15 regimental commander.

After the allied landings in Sicily Heilmann and his regiment parachuted into the Catania Plain to reinforce "Battle Group Schmalz" of the Hermann Göring Panzer Division. His battalions fought near Francoforte and Centuripe near Regalbuto, Bronte and Maletto. On December 1, 1943 Heilmann was promoted to Oberst.

On the Italian mainland Heilmann's regiment fought near Ortona, where on December 15 it ran into an assembly of enemy forces. His I and II Battalions (*Major* Böhmler and *Hauptmann* Liebscher) took Villa Grande. Ortona was held until December 28.

Heilmann's regiment also took part in the defensive battle at Monte Cassino. The third battle of Cassino saw it in the focal point of the battle for the monastery mountain.

On November 17, 1944 Ludwig Heilmann became commanding officer of the 5th Parachute Division, which subsequently fought in the Ardennes. Heilmann was captured by the Americans just prior to the end of the war and was released in 1947.

ERICH HELLMANN

Born on February 13, 1916 in Lörzen, East Prussia.
Ultimate rank: Oberleutnant.
Last service position: Commander of 1st Company, 3rd Parachute Regiment.
German Cross in Gold on August 2, 1943.
Knight's Cross on September 30, 1944 as commander of 1st Company, 3rd Parachute Regiment with the rank of Leutnant.
Erich Heilmann was assigned to I Battalion, 1st Flak Regiment in Königsberg, East Prussia on March 17, 1938.

Hellmann passed through the various stations of his career as a soldier without attracting undue attention. He saw action in Russia with his regiment as a *Feldwebel* and *Oberfeldwebel*. On November 1, 1943, while serving with 1st Company, 3rd Parachute Regiment, he was promoted to *Leutnant* for bravery in the face of the enemy. After dozens of reconnaissance and combat patrols, surprise raids and other individual acts, Hellmann was awarded the German Cross in Gold on August 2, 1943.

During the 1st Parachute Division's action in the Cassino area from February 1, 1944, Erich Hellmann served in Battle Group Schulz and defended the mountain massif from the monastery to Hill 593, Calvary Mountain. After February 18 the Schulz Regiment was located between the 4th Parachute Regiment and the sector held by the 5th Mountain Infantry Division. When the Third Battle of Cassino began on May 11, 1944, the 1st Parachute Regiment was division reserve and was deployed south of the Via Casilina to guard the division's flank. The men of the 1st Parachute Division fought a defensive battle between Aquino and Monte Cassino against the British 6th Armored Division until May 24, when the retreat was finally begun. By May 28 the British division had taken Monte Grande in spite of bitter resistance by the 1st Parachute Regiment. The division subsequently defended Arce, covering the retreat by LI Mountain Infantry Corps.

Leutnant Hellmann and his unit fought as the rearguard in this area of operations, allowing the division to withdraw through Arce, Frosinone and Alatri to Subjaco.

In recognition of his accomplishments Hellmann was awarded the Knight's Cross on September 30, 1944.

Promoted to *Oberleutnant* on January 1, 1945, Hellmann was still in Italy when the war ended and was taken prisoner by the British.

HARRY HERRMANN

Born on May 27, 1909 in Berlin.
Ultimate rank: Oberst.
Last service position: Acting commander of the 9th Parachute Division.
German Cross in Gold on July 22, 1944.
Knight's Cross on July 9, 1941 as commander of 5th Company, 1st Parachute Regiment with the rank of Oberleutnant.

Harry Herrmann entered the Brandenburg-Havel Police School as a police cadet on April 3, 1929, beginning his military career in the same way as many later officers of the parachute troops.

On April 1, 1933 he joined 1st Company, Police Battalion Wecke. When the latter unit became part of the Luftwaffe on January 21, 1934, Herrmann became a member of 1st Company, General Göring State Police Group and on October 1, 1934 was sent to the Eiche Police Officer School near Potsdam. On October 1, 1935 he joined the officer ranks, becoming a *Leutnant.*

Herrmann took part in the second course given by the Stendal Parachute School. By October 1, 1937 he had advanced to become adjutant of I Battalion, General Göring Regiment and was promoted to *Oberleutnant* on January 1, 1938. Herrmann became adjutant of the 1st Parachute Regiment on January 1, 1939, and on August 1 he became an ordnance officer in the headquarters of the 7th Air Division.

Hermann's first action in the Second World War was the airborne invasion of Fortress Holland. He won both Iron Crosses in Holland and on June 1, 1940 was appointed commander of 5th Company, 1st Parachute Regiment in Tangermünde.

Herrmann parachuted into Crete with 5th Company. Near Karteros, in the vicinity of the company's objective of Heraklion, he was wounded in the head while hanging beneath his parachute and was temporarily blinded. This limited Herrmann's actions. Led by his senior NCO Alfred Kurth and his orderly, who were killed at his side in the course of the fighting, Herrmann reached the vicinity of the airfield. Herrmann provided his company with a shining example. On July 9, 1941 he was decorated with the Knight's Cross. Herrmann was promoted to *Major* on April 1, 1942. On May 1 he went to XI Fliegerkorps as Ia. Appointed commander of the newly-formed Parachute Instruction Regiment, he led the unit in the action near Anzio-Nettuno.

Herrmann and his unit were named in the Wehrmacht communique on April 5, 1944. August 1 saw his promotion to *Oberstleutnant.* Until the end of the war Herrmann saw action with the Parachute Anti-tank Battalion "Herrmann."

Herrmann was held prisoner by the Soviets from May 2, 1945 to October 9, 1955.

MAX HERZBACH

Born on January 17, 1914 in Berlin-Drewitz.
Ultimate rank: Major.
Last service position: Commander of II Battalion, 7th Parachute Regiment in Brest.
German Cross in Gold on July 23, 1944.
Knight's Cross on September 13, 1944 as commander of 7th Company, 7th Parachute Regiment with the rank of Hauptmann.

Herzbach joined the 9th Prussian Infantry Regiment "Potsdam" on November 1, 1932. On April 1, 1938 he reported to the army's parachute-rifle battalion and on October 1 of that year went to 5th Company, 1st Parachute Regiment in Braunschweig.

Herzbach saw action in Poland and Holland, but it was not until February 16, 1942, when he joined the 6th Company, 2nd Parachute Regiment as a *Feldwebel* and platoon leader, that he found his home as a soldier. Under *Oberst* Sturm he jumped at the Corinth Canal and on June 25, 1941 was decorated with the Iron Cross, First Class. Exactly one month earlier he had been badly wounded after heavy fighting in Crete. Herzbach did not return to his unit until October 23, 1942. This followed a promotion to *Leutnant* on August 1 of that year.

Herzbach took over a platoon of the 8th Company, 2nd Parachute Regiment. He was promoted to *Oberleutnant* on November 1, 1942 and with his regiment fought as part of the 2nd Parachute Division under Generalleutnant Ramcke in Russia between Kiev and Kirovograd. Herzbach became commander of 10th Company, 2nd Parachute Regiment on July 22, 1943. Exactly one year later he received an early promotion to *Hauptmann* for bravery in the face of the enemy.

Max Herzbach saw action in Normandy with the 2nd Parachute Division. There was heavy fighting, first in the approaches of Brest, then in the fortress itself. The Americans were repulsed near Huelgoat, losing 32 tanks. In the course of the fighting II Battalion, 7th Parachute Regiment was overrun by the enemy and taken to Braspart by French resistance fighters. *Leutnant* Erich Lepkowski led a daring night raid which freed the captives.

Herzbach, a *Major* since September 1, 1944, and his 7th Company defended Fortress Brest with great determination. Herzbach was badly wounded again and on September 13 was decorated with the Knight's Cross. Captured by the Americans on September 19, 1944, he was released on March 7, 1946.

FRIEDRICH AUGUST FREIHERR VON DER HEYDTE

Born on March 30, 1907 in Munich.
Ultimate rank: Oberstleutnant.
Last service position: Commander of Battle Group von der Heydte in the Ardennes.
German Cross in Gold on March 9, 1942.
Knight's Cross on July 9, 1941 as commander of I Battalion, 3rd Parachute Regiment with the rank of Hauptmann.
Oak Leaves (617th recipient) on October 18, 1944 as commander of the 6th Parachute Regiment with the rank of Oberstleutnant.

Von der Heydte joined the Reichswehr as an officer candidate on April 1, 1925. He served in the 18th Cavalry Regiment, then in the 2nd Cavalry Regiment in Allenstein. On April 5, 1937 he became the commander of 2nd Company, 6th Anti-tank Battalion in Herford with the rank of *Oberleutnant.*

Von der Heydte fought in the Western Campaign as an infantry *Hauptmann.* He reported to the parachute troops on August 1, 1940 and passed the parachutist-rifleman course. On October 25, 1940 he was promoted to *Hauptmann* and became commander of I Battalion, 3rd Parachute Regiment on December 10. *Hauptmann* von der Heydte and his battalion parachuted into Crete and on May 20, 1941 occupied Agya penitentiary. In the days that followed his forces tied down a numerically far-superior force near Peribolia and Pyrgos. On May 25 he led his battalion in an attack over the Alikianou-Chania road. Von der Heydte and his battalion took possession of the east end of the Cretan capital on May 27 and pushed on to the harbor. On August 1, 1941 von der Heydte was promoted to *Major.*

Major von der Heydte fought successfully in North Africa as the leader of Battle Group von der Heydte, part of the Ramcke Brigade.

On February 1, 1943 he became Ia of the 2nd Parachute Division. While flying over Elba the aircraft carrying von der Heydt crashed. Seriously injured, von der Heydte was put out of action for more than four months.

Von der Heydte became commanding officer of the newly-formed 6th Parachute Regiment on February 1, 1944. During the enemy landings in Normandy his regiment wiped out an enemy parachute detachment. he and his regiment were named in the Wehrmacht communique.

Promoted to *Oberstleutnant* on August 1, 1944, von der Heydte was assigned to set up the parachute army's combat school in Aalten. On December 8, 1944 he formed Battle Group von der Heydte, which parachuted into the Ardennes during the night of December 17, 1944 "to open and keep open bottlenecks for the Sixth SS-Panzer Army." Success eluded the battle group. *Oberstleutnant* von der Heydte was wounded and taken prisoner by the Americans on December 24. He was released on July 12, 1947.

EDUARD GEORG HÜBNER

Born on April 16, 1914 in Hinzweiler, Cusel District.
Ultimate rank: Hauptmann.
Last service position: Commander of the First Parachute Army's assault battalion.
German Cross in Gold on June 21, 1943.
Knight's Cross on March 17, 1945 as commander of the First Parachute Army's assault battalion with the rank of Hauptmann.

Georg Hübner joined the 7th (Bavarian) Motor Transport Battalion, Fürth as an officer candidate on October 1, 1934 and became a *Fahnenjunker* on April 1, 1935. After attending Hannover Officer Candidate School he went to I Battalion, 5th Flak Regiment, Munich, where he was promoted to *Leutnant* on April 20, 1940.

Transferred to the General Göring Airborne (Glider) Battalion on April 1, 1938, Hübner took part in the Sudeten action and on November 1, 1938 was named adjutant of the 51st Flak Regiment based in Stettin. He transferred to the parachute troops on February 1, 1940 and was sent to Wittstock parachute school.

On March 1, 1940 Hübner became a platoon leader in 1st Company, 1st Parachute Regiment in Stendal. He saw action in Poland and at Narvik. Hübner won the Iron Cross, First Class in Crete. On November 13, 1941 he was wounded while serving in Russia.

Hübner was assigned to 16th Company, 1st Parachute Replacement Regiment in Stendal on December 20, 1941 and subsequently became the adjutant of I Battalion, 4th Parachute Regiment. On April 25, 1942 he was appointed leader of the regiment's pioneer platoon. Hübner became commander of 11th Company, 4th Parachute Regiment on July 1, 1942 and on November 1 was promoted to *Oberleutnant.*

Hübner served a second tour of duty in Russia in the Smolensk area. In Sicily he won the German Cross in Gold. *Oberleutnant* Hübner participated in the defensive battles from Reggio to Casino. On February 1, 1944 he was entrusted with II Battalion, 4th Parachute Regiment, having been promoted to *Hauptmann* on November 1, 1943 for bravery in the face of the enemy.

Hauptmann Hübner fought in the Wesel-Xanten area with the First Parachute Army's assault battalion and on March 2, 1945 prevented an enemy breakthrough and the premature loss of this bridgehead. Hüner's actions allowed the German forces to withdraw east across the Rhine. On March 17, 1945 he was awarded the Knight's Cross.

Hübner was held by the British as a prisoner of war from May 8, 1945 to July 31, 1947.

GEORG RUPERT JACOB

Born on September 29, 1915 in Kronbusch, Westphalia.
Ultimate rank: Oberleutnant.
Last service position: Commander of 1st Company, 7th Parachute Regiment.
Knight's Cross on September 13, 1944 as commander of 1st Company, 7th Parachute Regiment with the rank of Oberleutnant.

Jacob joined the 25th Motorized Infantry Regiment on November 1, 1938. He reported to the parachute troops on June 1, 1940 and on September 1 was assigned to the 16th Parachute Replacement Battalion in Stendal.

Jacob fought with I Battalion, 7th Parachute Regiment in the Russian Campaign and was decorated with the Iron Cross, First Class on June 25, 1942. On August 1 he was promoted to *Leutnant* for bravery in the face of the enemy.

He subsequently saw action in Normandy with the 2nd Parachute Division as an *Oberleutnant* and commander of 1st Company. The 2nd Parachute Division had been encircled by the enemy near Falaise. The encircling ring had to be cracked. The 7th Parachute Regiment was marching from Sizun across the Commana toward Huelgoat to do just that when it was attacked by American tanks on August 6.

During the struggle French partisans attacked from ambush. I Battalion was encircled. Only a part of the battalion under *Major* Becker managed to fight its way free. Nevertheless the regiment held for 72 hours before withdrawing to the hills of the Mons d'Arree, which were likewise held. Not until August 9 were the paratroops forced to withdraw into the approaches to Brest.

For 1st Company, 7th Parachute Regiment the final battle in Brest's system of tunnels and bunkers became a desperate struggle. *Oberleutnant* Jacob distinguished himself repeatedly. He and his men held the main barricade on Espagnol Peninsula and twice threw the enemy back. Finally *General* Ramcke surrendered. Georg Jacob and his comrades became prisoners of war but were released in 1946.

DR. ROLF KARL ERNST JÄGER

Born on November 1, 1912 in Klein Kunterstein, Graudenz District.
Ultimate rank: Oberstabsarzt.
Last service position: Director of the military hospital in Tarvis.
Knight's Cross on May 15, 1940.
Died on January 6, 1984 in Hagen, Westphalia.

Rolf Jäger applied to join the Reichsheer on September 15, 1934 and was assigned to the 6th Prussian First-aid Battalion of the 6th Infantry Division. After passing his physical on October 26, 1934, he joined the Giessen Infantry Regiment on April 1, 1934. Jäger attended the Berlin Military Medical Academy in November-December and on November 1, 1935 transferred to the Luftwaffe.

Jäger served at the Berlin-Gatow School of Air Warfare from February 24 to March 31, 1936. He subsequently joined the Luftwaffe Sport School and while there completed his 11th semester in medicine in Berlin.

On January 5 Jäger was promoted to *Unterarzt* and joined the 6th Air District First-aid Battalion in Münster. He was promoted to *Arzt* on December 21, 1938 and *Oberarzt* on February 16, 1939.

Jäger was transferred to the Koch Parachute Assault Battalion on February 23, 1940 and took part in the airborne assault on the Albert Canal bridges. He landed with the battalion staff near the Vroenhoven Bridge. Immediately after landing Dr. Jäger set about treating those paratroopers injured on landing or wounded in the air. Jäger and his assistants successfully recovered the bodies of the seven men of the battalion who were killed and treated 24 wounded, under heavy fire and at great personal risk. In recognition of his actions Jäger was awarded both Iron Crosses on May 12 and 13 and the Knight's Cross on May 15, 1940.

Promotion to *Stabsarzt* came on May 20, 1940. During the airborne invasion of Crete, Jäger, now battalion medical officer of the Parachute Assault Regiment's I Battalion, once again gave his all in caring for his wounded comrades. He continued to serve as a medical officer in Russia, where he was promoted to *Oberstabsarzt*. At Anzio-Nettuno and in Northern Italy, where he was director of Tarvis Military Hospital, Jäger dedicated himself to the recovery of the wounded placed in his care. He was taken prisoner by the British on May 8, 1945 and was released on January 20, 1947.

SIEGFRIED JAMROWSKI

Born on November 1, 1917 in Angerapp, East Prussia.
Ultimate rank: Major.
Last service position: Commander of III Battalion, 3rd Parachute Regiment.
German Cross in Gold on March 29, 1944.
Knight's Cross on June 9, 1944 as commander of 6th Company, 3rd Parachute Regiment with the rank of Oberleutnant.

Jamrowski joined I (Light Infantry) Battalion, 2nd Infantry Regiment in Ortelsburg, East Prussia on October 1, 1936. On October 25, 1938 he left the service with the rank of *Feldwebel* in order to study forestry. When mobilization was ordered Jamrowski was called up by the 2nd Infantry Regiment and served at the infantry school in Döberitz, instructing Austrian officer candidates. He was later employed as an infantry instructor, before he joined the parachute troops on June 1, 1940. Jamrowski completed the parachute course at Wittstock and on September 1, 1940 became a platoon leader in 8th Company, 3rd Parachute Regiment as a *Leutnant.*

Jamrowski fought in Russia in the winter of 1941 and on December 12 received the Iron Cross, First Class.

On February 24, 1942 Jamrowski became adjutant of IV Battalion, 3rd Parachute Regiment. He was promoted to *Oberleutnant* on April 1, became a platoon leader in the regiment's 6th Company and saw action in Sicily. Jamrowski was made commander of 6th Company on December 17, 1943 and fought on the Italian mainland. *Oberleutnant* Jamrowski was in the thick of the fighting in the Battle of Monte Cassino. In February 20, 1944 he and his company relieved the 211th Grenadier Regiment in Cassino city.

In the defensive battle Jamrowski led the 6th and 8th Companies simultaneously. His 6th Company lay at the edge of a tremendous bombardment. When the enemy attack began he opened fire on the attacking New Zealanders and held his sector of the city. *Oberleutnant* Jamrowski and his battalion commander, *Major* Foltin, received the Knight's Cross. On May 1, 1944 Jamrowski was promoted to *Hauptmann* and on June 15 became commander of IV Battalion.

In January 1945 Jamrowski was made commander of III Battalion, 3rd Parachute Regiment. He led the unit until the end of the war. On March 28, 1945 Jamrowski was promoted to *Major* for bravery in the face of the enemy.

WILHELM KEMPKE

Born on November 15, 1920 in Lulendorf, Güstrow District, Pomerania.
Ultimate rank: Oberleutnant.
Last service position: Leader of the technical echelon of KG 200.
Knight's Cross on August 21, 1941 as a squad leader in 1st Company, Parachute Assault Regiment with the rank of Feldwebel.
Killed on December 2, 1944 during a flight over German territory.

Wilhelm Kempke joined the Luftwaffe as a volunteer on July 1, 1938. He was assigned to 3rd Company, 1st Parachute Assault Regiment and underwent parachutist-rifleman training in Stendal. As a member of the Koch Parachute Assault Battalion Kempke took part in the attack on Eben Emael, where he distinguished himself through his boldness and daring. He was awarded the Iron Cross, First Class on May 25, 1940.

In Crete Kempke fought as a member of the Koch Battalion's 1st Company commanded by *Oberleutnant* Genz. There the company was given a special mission: eliminate a heavy flak battery south of Chania. When *Oberleutnant* Kellner, commander of the company headquarters platoon, was killed, Kempke assumed command of the platoon and captured the battery.

Kempke was awarded the Knight's Cross for his actions in Crete. He received the decoration from Göring himself, who personally promoted Kempke to *Oberfeldwebel*. (Later his promotion to *Feldwebel* was backdated to August 17, 1940).

In Russia Kempke was promoted to *Leutnant* on August 1, 1942 and exactly one year later, on August 1, 1943, to *Oberleutnant*.

On March 22, 1943 Kempke reported to Pilot School A/B 1 in Görlitz before joining KG 200, a recently formed special unit which was to investigate the use of Go 242 W gliders against enemy warships. On November 17, 1943 he became leader of the technical echelon of II./KG 200. He was killed in an airplane crash on December 2, 1944 during a flight over German territory.

HORST KERFIN

Born on March 21, 1913 in Insterburg, East Prussia.
Ultimate rank: Hauptmann.
Last service position: Commander of 5th Company and adjutant of the 1st Parachute Regiment (Oberst Karl-Lothar Schulz).
Knight's Cross on May 24, 1940 as a platoon leader in 11th Company, 1st Parachute Regiment with the rank of Oberleutnant.
Killed in action on January 22, 1943 near Alexeyevka, Orel area.

Horst Kerfin joined the Reichswehr's 12th Infantry Regiment on March 30, 1932 and underwent the standard infantry training.

On October 1, 1935 he transferred to the Luftwaffe and in early 1937 received parachutist-rifleman training. Kerfin joined the General Göring Airborne (Glider) Battalion (which soon afterward became III Battalion, 3rd Parachute Regiment) as an *Unteroffizier* on April 1, 1938. On June 1, 1938 he was promoted to *Feldwebel*.

Kerfin saw action in Poland as a *Feldwebel* and on October 29, 1939 was decorated with the Iron Cross, Second Class. On December 28, 1939 he was promoted to *Oberleutnant* (Kerfin skipped the rank of *Leutnant* with a retroactive service date of April 1, 1937).

Oberleutnant Kerfin took part in the invasion of Holland as a member of III Battalion, 1st Parachute Regiment. He was given a special mission in the battalion's assault on Rotterdam's Waalhaven airport on May 10, 1940. He and his platoon jumped near Feyenoord, stormed through the village and commandeered a streetcar, which they drove to a point just short of their objective, the Maas island in the southeast part of the city. His platoon silenced the enemy anti-aircraft guns, advanced across the Willems Bridge and established a bridgehead on the north bank of the river, which was held until other German troops arrived. Kerfin was awarded the Knight's Cross.

Kerfin, who had been promoted to *Hauptmann* on August 1, 1944, also made a name for himself in Russia. He was killed in battle near Alexeyevka, in the Orel area, on January 22, 1943.

HELLMUT KERUTT

Born on August 19, 1916 in Johannisburg, East Prussia.
Ultimate rank: Major.
Last service position: Commander of an instructional group (after being badly wounded) at the Parachute Officer School in Berlin-Reinickendorf, later Goslar.
German Cross in Gold on November 14, 1943.
Knight's Cross on February 2, 1945 as commander of the Kerutt Parachute Battalion with the rank of Major.

Hellmut Kerutt joined the 7th Flak Regiment's 2nd Company as an officer candidate on April 6, 1936 and subsequently completed an auxiliary observer course at Oldenburg Flying School. On June 1, 1937 he went to III Luftwaffe Officer Candidate School in Wildpark-Werder and became a *Leutnant* on January 1, 1938. After two postings to flak units, the second as adjutant of the 841st Light Flak Battalion, on July 28, 1940 he reported to Braunschweig Parachute School for parachutist-rifleman training and on August 15 became adjutant of the 7th Parachute Flak Battalion.

Kerutt became a platoon leader in the 2nd Battery of the 7th Parachute Flak Battalion on November 20, 1940 and on April 26, 1941 was made company commander of 2nd Company, Parachute Machine-gun Flak Battalion.

Kerutt was put to the test in the heavy fighting in Crete and was wounded on May 21. He won both Iron Crosses.

On December 15, 1942 Kerutt was wounded again, this time in Russia, and on June 15, 1942 was transferred to the officer reserve of IV Battalion, Parachute Reserve Regiment. There he was promoted to *Hauptmann* on September 19, 1942.

Kerutt returned to Russia as commander of 1st Company, 100th Luftwaffe Field Battalion. On January 15, 1943 he was placed in command of the 100th Battalion, which was also known as the Special Purpose Parachute Battalion. Further postings followed.

While serving in Russia with the 2nd Parachute Anti-tank Battalion, whose commander he became on December 2, 1943, Kerutt won the German Cross in Gold.

Promoted to *Major* on March 1, 1944, on June 8 of that year Kerutt became commanding officer of II Battalion, 7th Parachute Regiment. On August 16 he was named commander of I Battalion, 18th Parachute Regiment (commanded by von Hoffmann).

In Holland the Kerutt Battalion was deployed to defend against an enemy attack. When strong armored forces broke through the German encircling ring on September 17, 1944, they were stopped by the Kerutt Battalion in bitter fighting.

October 16 saw Kerutt at the head of his battalion and two days later a battle group, in defensive fighting in the Vernraij area. He was seriously wounded while leading a successful counterattack. This won Kerutt the Knight's Cross.

KARL KOCH

Born on March 19, 1920 in Bildenstein, Rhineland.
Ultimate rank: Oberfeldwebel.
Last service position: Assault platoon leader in III Battalion, 15th Parachute Regiment.
German Cross in Gold on August 2, 1943.
Knight's Cross on October 24, 1944 as leader of an assault platoon in III Battalion, 15th Parachute Regiment with the rank of Oberfeldwebel.
Killed in action on July 26, 1944 on the invasion front in Normandy.

Karl Koch joined the 11th Infantry Regiment's 6th Company as an eighteen-year-old volunteer on October 1, 1938 after completing his period of labor service. He took part in the fighting in Poland with his regiment. In the western campaign Koch was awarded the Iron Cross, Second Class. On September 17, 1941 he received the Iron Cross, First Class while serving in Russia and on November 1 was promoted to *Unteroffizier*.

Koch subsequently joined the parachute troops and on April 1, 1942 was assigned to 16th Company, 1st Parachute Regiment in Stendal. On November 1, 1942 he was promoted to *Feldwebel* and became a platoon leader in III Battalion, 1st Parachute Regiment, with which he saw action in the central sector of the Eastern Front near Smolensk and Orel in the winter of 1942/43. There he won the German Cross in Gold after leading numerous reconnaissance and combat patrols. On December 15, 1943 Koch was promoted to *Oberfeldwebel* for bravery in the face of the enemy.

Karl Koch stood the test in action in Italy. He also performed well in the west as an *Oberfeldwebel* and assault platoon leader in III Battalion, 15th Parachute Regiment, commanded by *Oberstleutnant* Gröschke.

On July 10, 1944 the 5th Parachute Division was moved from the Rennes area into the defensive front on the Cotentin Peninsula. When the division arrived in St. Lô, its individual regiments were placed under the command of various infantry units to prop up the front. *Oberstleutnant* Gröschke led his 15th Parachute Regiment into the 353rd Infantry Division's combat zone west of Carentan, where it defended positions astride the La Haye du Puits – Lessay road and in the Foret de Castre-Desert. *Oberfeldwebel* Koch played a leading role in the German defensive effort, leading his assault platoon as it eliminated enemy penetrations and closed gaps in the front.

Koch was killed in battle on July 26, 1944 and was posthumously awarded the Knight's Cross.

WALTER KOCH

Born on September 10, 1910 in Bonn.
Ultimate rank: Oberstleutnant.
Last service position: Officer Reserve of the Reich Minister of Aviation and Commander-in-Chief of the Luftwaffe.
German Cross in Gold on April 20, 1942.
Knight's Cross on May 10, 1940 as commander of the Koch Parachute Assault Battalion with the rank of Hauptmann.
Died in hospital in Berlin on October 23, 1943.

Walter Koch joined the police service on April 3, 1929 and in August 1935 was taken into the Luftwaffe. Initially he served as a *Leutnant* in the state police, and from September 1, 1935 as company officer in I (Light Infantry) Battalion, General Göring Regiment with the rank of *Oberleutnant.* Koch completed the parachute-rifle course in Stendal on September 26, 1936. On September 1, 1937 he became a company officer in IV (Parachute-Rifle) Battalion, General Göring Regiment and on April 1, 1938 took over 1st Company, 1st Parachute Regiment as company commander.

Koch was promoted to *Hauptmann* on April 20. In Hildesheim he oversaw the formation of the Koch Parachute Assault Battalion, which was to carry out special tasks in the campaign in the west.

The assault battalion saw its first action on May 10, 1940. Koch himself played a leading role in planning the assault on the Belgian fortress of Eben Emael. His assault battalion, which also captured the four bridges over the Albert Canal, successfully carried out all the tasks assigned to it. Walter Koch and ten other officers and men of his unit received the Knight's Cross.

On May 20, 1941 the Koch Assault Battalion, now designated I Battalion, 1st Parachute Assault Regiment, went into action in Crete. At 07.25 hours on the first day of the invasion Koch suffered a serious head wound in fighting near Hill 107.

Koch was named commander of the 5th Parachute Regiment on March 11, 1942 and led the unit in Tunisia. In January 1943 his regiment was incorporated into the Hermann Göring Panzer Division as the Light Infantry Regiment HG.

Walter Koch, who had been promoted to *Oberstleutnant* on April 20, 1942, fell ill in Tunisia and had to be transferred to a German hospital.

Koch joined the officer reserve on August 28, 1943. He was involved in a serious accident and died of his injuries in a Berlin hospital on October 23, 1943.

WILLI KOCH

Born on December 1, 1916 in Breslau, Silesia.
Ultimate rank: Hauptmann.
Last service position: Commander of 3rd Company, 1st Parachute Regiment.
Knight's Cross on June 9, 1944 as leader of 2nd Platoon, 3rd Company, 1st Parachute Regiment with the rank of Oberfeldwebel.

Willi Koch went straight to the 1st (Parachute) Regiment General Göring as a volunteer, joining the unit in Berlin-Charlottenburg on November 1, 1936.

On April 1, 1938 Koch was transferred to the 1st Parachute Regiment's 1st Company in Stendal. After completing an NCO course, on October 1, 1938 Koch was transferred to 3rd Company. There he received a promotion to *Oberjäger* and on June 1, 1940, after completing squad leader and pioneer courses, was promoted to *Feldwebel*.

Koch participated in the Polish Campaign and twice saw action in Norway. His second action there was a parachute drop to relieve the German forces fighting near Narvik. Between the two Norwegian actions he fought in Fortress Holland with 3rd Company and won both Iron Crosses.

As a platoon leader in 3rd Company Koch emerged unscathed from the hell of Crete. He twice saw action in Russia with his regiment and was promoted to *Oberfeldwebel* on January 1, 1943.

In Italy Koch served as leader of the 2nd Platoon of the 3rd Company, 1st Parachute Regiment, part of the battle group commanded by *Oberst* Schulz in the Battle of Monte Cassino. Koch and his platoon were right in the thick of things at Cassino and played a decisive role in repulsing an assault by elite British units between the left boundary, the abbey, and the right boundary, Hill 593 (Calvary Mountain).

Bitter fighting developed between the German paratroops and British gurkha troops and a battalion of the Sussex Light Infantry in brush-covered terrain where visibility was limited to about ten meters. If the enemy had broken through there it would have become impossible to hold the Cassino front.

Willi Koch received the Knight's Cross and on June 1, 1944 was promoted to *Leutnant* for bravery in the face of the enemy. This was followed by his promotion to *Oberleutnant* on October 1, 1944. On May 1, 1945 Koch was promoted to *Hauptmann* while commanding 3rd Company, 1st Parachute Regiment.

RUDOLF KRATZERT

Born on April 25, 1898 in Karlsburg, Siebenbürgen.
Ultimate rank: Major.
Last service position: Commander of the 3rd Parachute Training and Replacement Regiment.
German Cross in Gold on October 27, 1943.
Knight's Cross on June 9, 1944 as commander of III Battalion, 3rd Parachute Regiment with the rank of Major.
Deceased (date unknown).

Kratzert joined the Imperial Austrian Army on January 2, 1916 and entered the Breitensee-Vienna Infantry Cadet School. During the First World War he saw action in the battle at the Piave as a *Leutnant*. Kratzert joined the postal service on April 1, 1920 and rose to the position of senior postal inspector.

On April 30, 1940 he was reactivated and placed at the disposal of the Luftwaffe. Kratzert participated in a Luftwaffe officers course in Kamenz, Saxony. On June 26, 1940 he became base company commander at Aibling airfield in Upper Bavaria.

Kratzert was promoted to *Hauptmann* on December 13, 1941 and on June 1 was transferred to the Luftwaffe officer reserve. On March 27, 1942 he was attached at his own request to the 3rd Parachute Regiment as special duties officer.

On June 25, 1942 he became company commander of 11th Company, 3rd Parachute Regiment and on February 15 commanding officer of III Battalion, 3rd Parachute Regiment. In October of that year Kratzert fought near Strynkovo, battled partisans near Tolkachi and finally participated in the defense against enemy attacks near Massejenki. He served in Russia from October 1942 to March 1943 and on May 25, 1943 received the Knight's Cross.

Kratzert's first parachute operation was in Sicily. He fought in the areas of Carlentini, Lentini and Fondaco, near Regalbuto, Bronte and Randazzo.

On the Italian mainland Kratzert and his battalion fought near Eboli and Potenza. In mid-October he repulsed heavy armored attacks against his positions near Montecilfone and Palato. A night assault by an Indian unit ten times stronger than his own was likewise turned back. In the Cassino battle zone Kratzert and his unit held a position on Hill 593. On February 10, 1944 he launched a surprise attack on Calvary Mountain. The mountain was taken after a two-hour battle and Kratzert was awarded the Knight's Cross.

Kratzert's final position was commanding officer of the 3rd Parachute Training and Replacement Regiment. On May 4, 1945 he was taken prisoner by the Soviets but was able to escape to Vienna.

HEINZ KRINK

Born on March 25, 1919 in Berlin-Charlottenburg.
Ultimate rank: Hauptmann.
Last service position: Adjutant of II Battalion, 3rd Parachute Regiment.
German Cross in Gold on March 6, 1944.
Knight's Cross on June 9, 1944.

Krink's service with the Luftwaffe's 2nd Construction Battalion began on August 26, 1939. Soon afterward he transferred to the parachute troops and was assigned to 6th Company, 1st Parachute Regiment. Beginning on September 1, 1941 he participated in Course 9 for wartime officer commissions at Officer Candidate School 2 in Berlin-Gatow.

Krink made *Oberjäger* on February 1, 1942 and on November 1, 1942 became a *Feldwebel* in the 3rd Parachute Regiment's pioneer platoon. He took part in the second phase of the parachute troops' tour of duty in Russia and was decorated with the Iron Cross, Second Class on March 17, 1943 and the Iron Cross, First Class on September 10. Krink was promoted to *Leutnant* on April 20, 1943.

Heinz Krink earned an excellent reputation in Russia in the course of many offensive patrol operations and became known in the regiment as "the duty offensive patrol leader." On February 20, 1944 II Battalion, 3rd Parachute Regiment relieved the 211th Grenadier Regiment in Cassino city. There Krink took part in the difficult Second Battle of Cassino, supporting his battalion commander, *Hauptmann* Foltin, in every possible way to ensure that Cassino could be held. Krink won the German Cross in Gold for his part in the fighting at Cassino.

In the Third Battle of Cassino *Major* Veth led the battalion in place of the wounded Foltin. It held a critical part of the front from Calvary Mountain to the Colle San Angelo.

During the German withdrawal Krink commanded the rearguard and was recommended for the Knight's Cross by the commander of the 1st Parachute Division, *Generalleutnant* Heidrich. He received the award on June 9, 1944. On April 20, 1944 Krink was promoted to *Hauptmann* for bravery in the face of the enemy during the fighting withdrawal in Northern Italy. Krink was taken prisoner on May 2, 1945.

HANS KROH

Born on May 13, 1907 in Heidelberg.
Ultimate rank: Generalmajor.
Last service position: Commander of the 2nd Parachute Division in Fortress Brest.
German Cross in Gold on December 24, 1942.
Knight's Cross on August 21, 1941 as commander of I Battalion, 2nd Parachute Regiment with the rank of Major.
Oak Leaves (442nd recipient) on April 6, 1944 as commander of the 2nd Parachute Regiment with the rank of Oberstleutnant.
Swords (96th recipient) on September 12, 1944 as commander of the 2nd Parachute Division with the rank of Oberst.
Died on July 18, 1967 in Braunschweig.

Kroh entered the Brandenburg-Havel Police School as a police cadet on April 8, 1926. On October 1, 1935 he became commander of 2nd Company, General Göring Regiment and transferred to the Luftwaffe on April 1, 1936. Kroh completed the parachutist-rifleman course and became training director of the Stendal Parachute School. After a period of staff work, on September 1, 1940 he assumed command of I Battalion, 2nd Parachute Regiment.

During the invasion of Crete Kroh took command of Battle Group Sturm, whose objective was Rethymnon airfield, after *Oberst* Sturm was taken prisoner by the British. Near Stavromenos and at the oil refinery the paratroops held out against a vastly superior enemy force. It was there that *Oberleutnant* Roon and his 3rd Company stormed the village of Kimari. Following a bitter ten-day struggle, which occupied a large portion of the British-Greek armed forces, the battle group was relieved by mountain infantry. Kroh received the Knight's Cross.

In Africa Kroh served as Ia of the Ramcke Brigade. It was he who initiated the brigade's escape through enemy territory following the German withdrawal after El Alamein.

In Russia Kroh and his regiment fought near Novo Andreyevka and Novgorodka. Near Butor the regiment eliminated a Russian bridgehead on the Dniepr. Kroh saw action at Kirovograd, where Russian attacks were repulsed.

Hans Kroh commanded the 2nd Parachute Division in the Battle of Brest until he was captured in the St. Pierre district of the city on September 18, 1944.

WILLY KROYMANNS

Born on April 9, 1920 in Kleve, Lower Rhine.
Ultimate rank: Oberleutnant.
Last service position: Commander of 5th Company, 12th Parachute Regiment and the Stendal Parachute Replacement Battalion.
Knight's Cross on January 20, 1945 as commander of 5th Company, 12th Parachute Regiment, 4th Parachute Division with the rank of Oberleutnant.

Kroymanns volunteered for military service and joined 1st Company, 1st Parachute Regiment in Stendal on October 1, 1938.

On April 15, 1939 Kroymanns reported to Quakenbrück airfield for pilot training. From July 1, 1940 he served as a fighter pilot in I./JG 53 and fought on the Channel Front.

In the course of his 64 combat sorties Kroymanns shot down six enemy aircraft and was awarded the Iron Cross, First Class on November 9, 1941.

After successfully passing senior NCO tests on November 28, 1942, Kroymanns returned to action and received the Day Fighter Operational Flying Clasp in Silver.

On November 1, 1943 Kroymanns took over the 1st Parachute Regiment's 2nd Company. Promoted to *Leutnant* on February 3, 1944, he was transferred to the 6th Parachute Regiment and on October 1, 1944 to 5th Company, 12th Parachute Regiment.

On the Italian mainland the 4th Parachute Division battled the American 34th Infantry Division, and as a member of the division Kroymanns took part in the slow retreat toward Bologna. In the heavy fighting against the hotly-pursuing enemy, the Allied forces were halted in the Bologna area and later in the Po Plain until the bulk of I Parachute Corps had crossed the Po.

Kroymanns fought in the rearguard, freed surrounded comrades and won the Knight's Cross.

Kroymanns subsequently saw action again, in the area of the Lower Rhine. He led his 5th Company, 12th Parachute Regiment in bitter defensive actions west of the Rhine and to the east as far as the Berlin area until the end.

Martin Kühne

Born on November 1, 1918 in Langebrück, Dresden District.
Ultimate rank: Major.
Last service position: Commander of I Battalion, 10th Parachute Regiment.
German Cross in Gold on July 23, 1943.
Knight's Cross on February 29, 1944 as commander of I Battalion, 2nd Parachute Regiment with the rank of Hauptmann.

Kühne joined I Battalion, 10th Flak Regiment in Dresden as an officer candidate on November 1, 1937. After attending officer candidate school in Fürstenfeldbruck, on September 1, 1939 Kühne went to Wittstock Parachute School as an *Oberfähnrich* and soon afterward was transferred to the 1st Parachute Regiment. On May 1, 1940 he was a *Leutnant* and platoon leader in 15th Company, 1st Parachute Regiment, with which he went into Fortress Holland. Deployed in the Moerdijk area, he was badly wounded while taking a heavily-fortified bunker. Kühne's actions in Holland were rewarded with the Iron Cross, First Class on May 18, 1940. During the action against the Corinth Canal and the airborne invasion of Crete Kühne led a platoon of 1st Company, 2nd Parachute Regiment. Near Corinth he captured a British anti-aircraft battery and took a large number of prisoners (which resulted in a recommendation for the Knight's Cross). In the invasion of Crete Kühne was dropped between the city and airport of Rethymnon. He and a handful of men defended their position and Kühne was badly wounded for the second time. He was subsequently awarded the Luftwaffe Honor Goblet.

Kühne arrived in Russia on October 1, 1941. There he served as adjutant and for a time commander of I Battalion, 2nd Parachute Regiment until November 1, 1942. Sent to Africa, he served with the Ramcke Brigade and played a part in that unit's successful escape through enemy-held territory. For his actions in Tunisia Kühne was awarded the German Cross in Gold.

Kühne saw action in Italy as commander of 4th Company, 2nd Parachute Regiment, before taking command of the regiment's I Battalion. On July 1, 1943 he was promoted to *Hauptmann*. Kühne and I Battalion were dropped over Leros, where British and Italian troops had joined forces, on November 12, 1943. There he won the Knight's Cross.

Kühne's battalion provided a cadre of personnel for the 10th Parachute Regiment, which fought in a defensive role from the Anzio-Nettuno beachhead to the last days in Italy in the Rovereto area. On March 1, 1945 he was promoted to *Major*.

KURT KUNKEL

Born on January 13, 1923 in Weiswasser, Oberlausitz.
Ultimate rank: Leutnant.
Last service position: Commander of 2nd Company, 4th Parachute Regiment.
Knight's Cross on April 30, 1945 as commander of 2nd Company, 4th Parachute Regiment with the rank of Leutnant.

Kurt Kunkel reported to the 63rd Luftwaffe Training Regiment in Straubling as a volunteer on November 1, 1940. He served in several positions before going to Braunschweig for jump training and the parachutist-rifleman course.

When the Battle of Sicily began Kunkel's regiment – the 4th Parachute Regiment commanded by *Oberstleutnant* Walther – was placed on alert. On the afternoon of July 14 Kunkel and his comrades parachuted into Sicily.

Kunkel was one of those NCOs of the parachute troops who did his duty wherever he was sent. In Sicily he saw action primarily in the area north of the Simeto and south of Catania, as well as in the subsequent retreat to the Italian mainland.

Kunkel was wounded during the fighting on the mainland and was forced to spend September and October in hospital. Following his release he saw action at Sulmena, Pizzo and Ferrato in the province of Abruzzi, and afterward at Orsogna-Ortona and in the Cassino area. There he led offensive patrols and his platoon formed the rearguard. On January 15, 1944 he received the Iron Cross, First Class.

From April to June 1944 Kunkel took part in a platoon leaders course in Central France. From there he was again forced to enter hospital and in August 1944 went to officer candidate school.

Following his promotion to *Leutnant* Kunkel took charge of 2nd Company, 4th Parachute Regiment and on April 20, 1945 was named company commander on orders from *Generalmajor* Schulz. Kunkel proved himself as a company commander during the retreat near Bologna and the fighting in the Po Plain. On April 30, 1945 he was awarded the Knight's Cross by *General* Heidrich. Kunkel was held by the British as a prisoner of war from May 3, 1945 to October 25, 1947.

RUDOLF KURZ

Born on January 29, 1916 in Kiel.
Ultimate rank: Leutnant.
Last service position: Platoon leader in I Battalion, 10th Parachute Regiment, 4th Parachute Division.
German Cross in Gold on July 12, 1943.
Wound Badge in Gold on September 24, 1944.
Knight's Cross on November 18, 1944 in the Bologna combat zone with the rank of Oberfähnrich.

Rudolf Kurz joined the German Armed Forces on February 1, 1938. He served in the army until 1940 and on July 7 was a *Feldwebel* and platoon leader in the 4th (Machine-gun) Company, 257th Infantry Regiment. He saw action with his company in France and was awarded the Iron Cross, Second Class. In 1941 he volunteered for service with the parachute troops. On June 18, 1941 Kurz received the Iron Cross, First Class for his actions during the invasion of Crete.

Kurz repeatedly distinguished himself while fighting in Russia with the 1st Parachute Regiment and on July 12, 1943 was awarded the German Cross in Gold. After his tour in Russia he joined the newly-formed 12th Parachute Regiment of the 4th Parachute Division in Italy.

After completing a wartime officer commission course Kurz became an *Oberfähnrich*. He led a platoon of 2nd Company, 12th Parachute Regiment during the bitter fighting by his division in the Green Position, which extended right across Italy from Viareggio on the Tyrrhenian Sea in the west to Rimini on the Adriatic.

The battle for the Futa Pass and in the area to the north saw Kurz in continuous action. September 20, 1944 marked the beginning of what became known among the German parachute troops as "the hard week," a battle for survival. These six days cost the 12th Parachute Regiment heavy sacrifices. The battalions fought the American 85th Infantry Division near Monte Altuzzo and Monticelli, east of Monte Verruca and west of Monte Altuzzo. The American advance toward Bologna and in the Po Plain was stopped for several weeks. Kurz, who had received the Wound Badge in Gold on September 24, 1944, distinguished himself repeatedly during the tank battle near Monghidoro and in the Battle of Pianoro. He was decorated with the Knight's Cross on November 18, 1944. On January 1, 1945 Kurz was promoted to *Leutnant*.

DR. CARL LAMGEMEYER

Born on August 6, 1907 in Holzminden, Lower Saxony.
Ultimate rank: Oberstabsarzt.
Last service position: Division Medical Officer, 2nd Parachute Division.
German Cross in Gold on March 20, 1944.
Knight's Cross on November 18, 1944 as commander of the Parachute First-aid Instruction Battalion of the parachute troops with the rank of Stabsarzt.
Died on July 25, 1982 in Holzminden.

Following graduation Carl Langemeyer studied medicine. A doctor of medicine at the outbreak of war, he joined the Luftwaffe as an *Assistenzarzt* and after the Polish Campaign joined the parachute troops as a medical officer.

In the invasion of Holland Langemeyer and his assistants jumped with the 1st Parachute Regiment near Dordrecht. There they had to operate and fight. This was only possible because parachute medical officers and first-aid personnel did not wear the red cross. At the end of this action Langemeyer was decorated with both Iron Crosses.

Dr. Langemeyer parachuted into Crete as commander of the 2nd Company, Parachute First-aid Battalion. In June he was awarded the Luftwaffe Honor Goblet for his actions in Crete.

In Russia Langemeyer led the 2nd Company of the Corps First-aid Battalion. Later he worked in the Luftwaffe hospital in Strassburg as senior medical officer, before becoming commander of the 1st Company, 2nd Parachute First-aid Battalion in Nimes on April 1, 1943. Langemeyer's actions in the Rome area in the period June-September 1943 resulted in the awarding of the German Cross in Gold.

On April 17, 1944 Dr. Langemeyer became the 1st Parachute Army's advising surgeon and on May 1, 1944 was made commanding officer of the Parachute First-aid Instruction Battalion in Nancy.

During the invasion of Normandy Langemeyer visited the front a number of times as advising surgeon. At the end of August his battalion was committed as an infantry battalion in the Nancy-Luneville area. He was wounded in the last attack on September 30, 1944. Langemeyer nevertheless continued to lead his battle group for three hours and repulsed all attacks. This won him the Knight's Cross. On November 1, 1944 Langemeyer was promoted to the rank of *Oberstabsarzt.* As Division Medical Officer of the 2nd Parachute Division he disbanded the units under his command in the Ruhr Pocket. On June 2, 1945 he arrived in Holzminden.

ERICH LEPKOWSKI

Born on September 17, 1919 in Giesen, East Prussia.
Ultimate rank: Oberleutnant.
Last service position: Commander of 5th Company, 2nd Parachute Regiment in Fortress Brest.
German Cross in Gold on December 25, 1943.
Knight's Cross on August 8, 1944 as a platoon leader in 5th Company, 2nd Parachute Regiment, Brest with the rank of Leutnant.
Died on May 31, 1974 in Saarbrücken.

Erich Lepkowski joined the 1st Infantry Regiment in Königsberg on January 1, 1938. After transferring to the Luftwaffe on September 1, 1939 he began training as a radio operator and on August 1, 1940 joined the regimental signals platoon of the 2nd Parachute Regiment in Berlin-Reinickendorf as radio section leader.

Since promoted to *Oberjäger*, Lepkowski took part in the parachute operation at Corinth Canal. He was taken prisoner in Crete, was freed and fought with the Rethymnon group of forces under *Major* Kroh, who was in command following the capture of *Oberst* Sturm.

In Russia Lepkowski, who was promoted to *Oberfeldwebel* on April 1, 1942, fought in the icy hell on the Mius, where he was decorated with the Iron Cross, First Class. In the swamps of the Volkhov he became "the duty patrol leader," with 30 offensive patrols in 48 days. In northern Russia Lepkowski was promoted to *Leutnant* for bravery in the face of the enemy.

Near Kirovograd Lepkowski served as adjutant of II Battalion, 2nd Parachute Regiment and later as commanding officer of 5th Company. He took part in a unique defensive battle on the hills near Pervomaisk, where his troops and three assault guns under his command repulsed several large-scale Soviet attacks. On December 25, 1943 he received the German Cross in Gold.

Near Novgorodka Lepkowski assumed command of 5th Company after *Oberleutnant* Nowarra was killed in action. In the period up to January 7, 1944 he and a total of 17 men fought off 16 attacks. Lepkowski was recommended for the Knight's Cross.

Lepkowski fought with equal zeal in Fortress Brest. In one legendary action he led an operation which liberated 113 comrades from the hands of French partisans. This was Lepkowski's finest hour and he was to have been decorated with the Oak Leaves. He was captured by the Americans on September 20, 1944, one of the last defenders of Fortress Brest to become a prisoner of war.

WALTER PAUL LIEBING

Born on August 12, 1912 in Dresden.
Ultimate rank: Oberstleutnant.
Last service position: Commander of the 25th Parachute Regiment.
Knight's Cross on February 2, 1945 as commander of the 23rd Parachute Regiment, 2nd Parachute Division with the rank of Major.

Liebing entered Meissen Police School as a police cadet on April 4, 1932. He took the officer candidate course at Dresden Police Headquarters and on February 1, 1933 became a platoon leader in the Dresden Police Department's 4th Hundertschaft.

After a series of appointments Liebing transferred to the Luftwaffe and on September 1, 1935 was promoted to *Leutnant*. He trained at various flight schools. On July 31, 1937 he became an *Oberleutnant*.

On November 30, 1940 Liebing assumed command of 1.(H)/32, a tactical reconnaissance unit, as *Staffelkapitän* and flew 32 sorties in the east. Liebing was awarded the Iron Cross, First Class on September 2, 1941. Promoted to *Hauptmann,* Liebing was assigned to the 1st Luftwaffe Field Division on September 1, 1942 and fought under *Generalmajor* Wilke in Russia. On February 1, 1943 he became a *Major* and was assigned to the First Parachute Army. It was anticipated that Liebing would become a battalion commander in the soon to be formed 6th Parachute Division.

Serving in Battle Group Eggers in the Nancy area, *Major* Liebing held the Mosel and Meurthe position as well as the Seulle sector against superior enemy forces. For these actions he was awarded the Knight's Cross.

On March 1, 1945 Liebing was placed in command of the 23rd Parachute Regiment. With this unit he stood his ground east of Krefeld, at Fischeln and near Gennep against enemy armored assaults and undertook a successful counterattack to liberate the commander of II Battalion, 23rd Parachute Regiment and his staff.

At the Rhine bridge at Uerdingen *Major* Liebing held a bridgehead until the last of his troops had crossed then blew the bridge on March 4, 1945.

Liebing was recommended for the Oak Leaves on March 10, 1945 but he did not receive the decoration. On April 26, 1945 he was taken prisoner by the Americans.

ROLF MAGER

Born on January 17, 1918 in Wuppertal.
Ultimate rank: Hauptmann.
Last service position: Commander of II Battalion, 6th Parachute Regiment.
German Cross in Gold on September 28, 1944.
Knight's Cross on October 31, 1944 as commander of II Battalion, 6th Parachute Regiment with the rank of Hauptmann.
Died on January 1, 1945 on the western front (died of his wounds in an American hospital).

Rolf Mager joined the Air Signals Replacement Battalion II./14 in Gütersloh on October 1, 1936. As a *Leutnant* he was assigned to the 13th Air District Signals Regiment in Nuremberg on August 1, 1938. From there he transferred to the parachute troops on January 1, 1941 and was assigned to the 1st Parachute Regiment.

Mager saw his first action in Crete as an *Oberleutnant.* He and the rest of 1st Parachute Regiment fought in the northern sector of the Eastern Front, where he won the Iron Cross, First Class on April 1, 1942.

After the Italian departure from the Axis alliance Mager and his regiment moved to Italy and fought initially in the southeast part of the mainland, subsequently seeing action during the fighting withdrawal to Rome and the north of the country.

On September 28, 1944 Mager received the German Cross in Gold after numerous actions warranting the Iron Cross, First Class.

Mager was promoted to *Major* and became commanding officer of II Battalion, 6th Parachute Regiment, 2nd Parachute Division on May 1, 1944. In September-October 1944 he and his unit fought at Schijndel and Alphen in a defensive role. His battalion stopped a strong armored attack then launched a nocturnal counterattack which drove the enemy infantry from the former German trenches. Mager established a new defensive line at Boxtel and thus stopped an enemy breakthrough to Tilburg. This won him the Knight's Cross. Mager was badly wounded and subsequently evacuated to Germany.

JOHANNES MARSCHOLEK

Born on February 13, 1917 in Gleiwitz, Upper Silesia.
Ultimate rank: Oberleutnant.
Last service position: Commander of 5th Company, 5th Parachute Flak Battalion (5th Parachute Division).
Knight's Cross on November 27, 1944 as commander of 5th Company, 5th Parachute Flak Battalion with the rank of Oberleutnant.

"Hannes" Marscholek joined 3rd Battery, 20th Flak Regiment in Breslau on November 4, 1936 after completing his required period of service with the Reich Labor Service (RAD). He was to remain with the flak throughout his career as a soldier.

Following a range-finder operator course and various transfers and postings, Marscholek, a *Wachtmeister* since October 1, 1938, joined the Linz Flak Battalion's 1st Battery as battery officer. On March 1, 1939 he became a *Leutnant* and as such saw action in the western campaign as commander of 3rd Battery, 371st Reserve Flak Battalion. On June 25, 1940 he and his battery were transferred to the home war zone to guard important installations. Marscholek was promoted to *Oberleutnant* there on January 23, 1942 and remained with the home defense until January 28, 1944. Marscholek received the Iron Cross, First Class after shooting down several enemy bombers.

On January 29, 1944 Marscholek became a member of the flak battalion designated for the 5th Parachute Division and became a platoon leader in 5th Battery, 5th Parachute Flak Battalion.

Marscholek led this battery in decisive phases of the defensive battle in Normandy. In two days his two flak eighty-eights knocked out 28 Sherman tanks on the Cotentin Peninsula and disabled four others. Of these Marscholek personally destroyed 21.

The villages of La Monts, Houteville, La Butte, Marigny, St. Lô and Avranches were the scenes of further success. When the battalion commander, *Major* Görtz, was killed in the fighting in La Oience on July 29, "Hannes" Marscholek took command. He was named in the Wehrmacht communique and won the Knight's Cross. He led the battalion until the final day of the war and went on to distinguish himself several more times.

EUGEN MEINDL

Born on July 16, 1892 in Donaueschingen.
Ultimate rank: General der Fallschirmtruppe.
Last service position: Commanding General of II Parachute Corps.
German Cross in Gold on July 27, 1942.
Knight's Cross on June 14, 1941 as commander of the 1st Parachute-Glider Regiment with the rank of Generalmajor.
Oak Leaves (564th recipient) on August 31, 1944 as General der Fallschirmtruppe and Commanding General of II Parachute Corps.
Swords (155th recipient) on May 8, 1945 as General der Fallschirmtruppe and Commanding General of II Parachute Corps.
Died on January 24, 1951 in Munich.

Eugen Meindl served with the artillery from July 27, 1912. In the First World War he commanded a platoon and later a battery and subsequently served as adjutant with the 67th Field Artillery Regiment and with the Artillery Commander, 52nd Corps.

Meindl served with various artillery units in the Reichswehr. Promoted to *Hauptmann* on August 1, 1924, on September 14, 1926 he was assigned to the Reichswehr Ministry and spent ten years there before being promoted to *Major.*

On November 10, 1939 *Oberstleutnant* Meindl was named commander of the 112th Mountain Artillery Regiment in Graz. As an *Oberst* he led the "Meindl Group" and made his very first parachute jump at Narvik. His transfer to the Luftwaffe followed on November 28, 1940, even though he had been commander of "Assault Regiment Meindl" of the parachute troops since August 9.

The airborne invasion of Crete saw Meindl jump near the Platanias Bridge, where he was shot through the chest, a very serious wound. *Major* Stentzler led the regiment until *Oberst* Ramcke arrived.

On February 26, 1942 *Generalmajor* Meindl became commander of the newly-formed Luftwaffe Division Meindl in Russia and on September 26 took over XII Fliegerkorps (later I Luftwaffe Field Corps).

Meindl distinguished himself in the winter fighting in Russia, was named in the Wehrmacht communique and on November 5, 1943 was promoted to commanding general of II Parachute Corps, which he led in the west on the invasion front and later at Cleve and in the Reichswald. Meindl's corps fought with distinction at Goch and in the Wesel bridgehead. Meindl was taken prisoner and held until September 29, 1947.

JOACHIM MEISSNER

Born on October 15, 1911 in Freystadt, Silesia.
Ultimate rank: Hauptmann.
Last service position: Commander of II Battalion, 2nd Parachute Regiment.
Knight's Cross on May 12, 1940 as acting commander of the Airborne (Glider) Group "Eisen" of the Koch Parachute Assault Battalion with the rank of Leutnant.
Killed in action on July 25, 1944 west of St. Lô, France.

Joachim Meissner joined the Reichswehr on October 1, 1929, having signed up for a twelve-year period of service. On April 1, 1934 he became Departmental Chief of the Foreign Section of the Reich Director of Sport under Hans von Tschammer und Osten, for southeast Europe.

With mobilization on August 26, 1939 Meissner was called up and joined the 8th Pioneer Battalion in Neisse as a *Feldwebel*.

Meissner transferred to the parachute troops on January 1, 1940. He was promoted to *Leutnant* in March and joined the Koch Parachute Assault Battalion.

As *Leutnant* Schächter's second in command Meissner flew with Assault Group "Eisen" to Canne. However the group arrived late and found that the enemy had already blown the bridge there.

After *Leutnant* Schächter was seriously wounded *Leutnant* Meissner assumed command of the group and occupied the village of Eben Emael. He defended this bridgehead against heavy enemy attacks until army troops arrived.

For this feat Meissner was awarded the Knight's Cross on May 12, 1940. On May 16 he received an early promotion to *Oberleutnant* for bravery in the face of the enemy.

Meissner took part in the parachute drops at the Corinth Canal and Crete with the 2nd Parachute Regiment. He fought in Russia at the Mius and the Volkhov.

On January 1, 1943 Meissner was assigned to XI Fliegerkorps as a staff officer. On April 16, 1944 he took over III Battalion, 14th (Motorized) Parachute Regiment and soon afterward II Battalion, 2nd Parachute Regiment. Meissner was killed in the battle for St. Lô on July 25, 1944.

OTTO MENGES

Born on May 9, 1917 in Bechtoldsheim, Oppenheim District, Rheinland-Pfalz.
Ultimate rank: Oberfeldwebel.
Last service position: Commander of 6th Company, 1st Parachute Regiment.
German Cross in Gold on March 20, 1944.
Knight's Cross on June 9, 1944 as commander of 6th Company, 1st Parachute Regiment with the rank of Oberfeldwebel.
Killed in action on May 24, 1944 in the battle zone north of Cassino.

Otto Menges joined IV (Parachute-Rifle) Battalion of the General Göring Regiment on October 1, 1937 and was taken into 2nd Company, 1st Parachute Regiment on April 1, 1938. After completing the parachutist-rifleman course in Stendal in the summer of 1938 and a pioneer course, Menges was promoted to *Oberjäger*.

Menges served with distinction in the Norwegian Campaign. He jumped with his unit into Crete, received the Iron Cross, First Class and on May 29 was captured by the British and held for a day.

Menges saw action in Russia twice. A Feldwebel since November 12, 1941, he was promoted to *Oberfeldwebel* in Russia on March 4, 1943. On October 18, 1943 his regimental commander, *Oberst* Schulz, submitted a recommendation for the German Cross in Gold, which Menges received on March 20, 1944.

Before receiving the decoration Menges was back in action, this time in the defensive battle in the Cassino area. There he led a counterattack by the depleted 6th Company, 1st Parachute Regiment and recaptured an important hill.

On February 11, 1944 the enemy drove into the German defensive positions between Hill 539 and the neighboring hills. *Oberfeldwebel* Menges once again seized the initiative and drove the enemy back in close-quarters fighting. Karl-Lothar Schulz submitted Menges for the Knight's Cross and recommended a promotion to *Leutnant* for bravery in the face of the enemy.

Menges was killed in action on May 24, 1944 while leading a counterattack north of Cassino.

GERHART MERTENS

Born on December 30, 1919 in Berlin.
Ultimate rank: Major.
Last service position: Commander of the 5th Parachute Pioneer Battalion.
German Cross in Gold on February 8, 1943.
Wound Badge in Gold on March 9, 1945.
Knight's Cross on December 6, 1944 as commander of the 5th Parachute Pioneer Battalion with the rank of Hauptmann.

Mertins joined the 208th Pioneer Replacement Company's 1st Platoon on September 7, 1939. By January 1, 1940 he had risen to become leader of the Company Headquarters Squad.

Mertins took part in the Balkans Campaign which began on March 17, 1941. He was promoted to *Leutnant* on April 30 and parachuted into Crete as a platoon leader in the Parachute Pioneer Battalion. Mertins was awarded the Iron Cross, First Class for his actions in Crete.

Leutnant Mertins went to the Eastern Front on October 1, 1941. There he took command of the battalion's 4th Company from the wounded *Oberleutnant* Gerstner and in the course of the fighting was himself wounded.

After recovering from his wounds Mertins was assigned to the headquarters of Luftflotte 3.

Mertins returned to the Eastern Front on October 28, 1942 and served there until January 30, 1943. Near Strasnogorodka his unit was encircled by Russian forces, but Mertins was able to break out of the encirclement. He fought at several critical points and was twice wounded. For his actions in Russia Mertins was awarded the German Cross in Gold.

From the Parachute Replacement Regiment in Stendal Mertins went to Cologne-Wahn, where he took over 1st Company, Parachute Pioneer Replacement Battalion on May 26, 1944.

Mertins commanded the 5th Parachute Division's 5th Parachute Pioneer Battalion during the retreat in Normandy and successfully brought his unit through to Nancy.

In subsequent actions he and his battalion blew 46 bridges and halted the pursuing enemy. For this he was awarded the Knight's Cross.

Mertins and his pioneer battalion helped save the 5th Parachute Division in the Ardennes. On March 9, 1945 Mertins was wounded for the fifth time.

HEINZ MEYER

Born on April 9, 1916 in Magdeburg.
Ultimate rank: Major.
Last service position: Commander of the 15th Parachute Regiment and leader of a battle group in the Harz Mountains.
German Cross in Gold on June 21, 1943.
Knight's Cross on April 8, 1944 as commander of III Battalion, 4th Parachute Regiment with the rank of Hauptmann.
Oak Leaves (654th recipient) on November 18, 1944 as commander of III Battalion, 15th Parachute Regiment with the rank of Hauptmann.

Meyer joined 14th (Parachute) Company, General Göring Regiment on November 2, 1937. On April 1, 1938 he joined 4th Company, 1st Parachute Regiment as a volunteer and on April 27, 1940 was assigned to the Luftwaffe Officer Candidate School in Berlin-Gatow. Meyer was promoted to *Leutnant* on August 1, 1940 and became a platoon leader in 11th Company, 3rd Parachute Regiment. Promoted to *Oberleutnant* on July 1, 1942, on December 22 he was placed in command of 11th Company, 4th Parachute Regiment.

Heinz Meyer took part in the parachute operations against Fortress Holland, fought in Norway under *Major* Walter and was awarded the Iron Cross, First Class on June 21, 1941 after the airborne invasion of Crete.

Meyer fought with equal bravado on the Leningrad Front as well as later at the Mius and the Volkhov.

Meyer's service in Italy began with the jump into Sicily. On November 1, 1943 he was promoted to *Hauptmann*. As interim commander of III Battalion, 3rd Parachute Regiment, Meyer led the unit in the defense of the notorious Calvary Mountain near Cassino. Following his return to 11th Company, on February 10, 1944 Meyer and the new battalion commander, *Major* Kratzert, recaptured Calvary Mountain, which had been taken by the enemy. Meyer was subsequently placed in command of III Battalion, 4th Parachute Regiment, with which he repulsed an attack by American tanks at Albaneta. Six enemy tanks were destroyed. Further tanks were destroyed using anti-tank mines and short-range weapons. Meyer and his regimental commander, *Major* Grassmehl, received the Knight's Cross.

In France Meyer led the 15th Parachute Regiment's III Battalion and stopped several American attacks near Monte Castre. There he won the Knight's Cross with Oak Leaves. Meyer was taken prisoner by the Americans in the Harz Mountains on May 8, 1945 but was released on December 20.

DR. WERNER MILCH

Born on November 15, 1903 in Wilhelmshaven.
Ultimate rank: Major.
Last service position: Commander of the Parachute Mortar Instruction Battalion.
German Cross in Gold on April 15, 1944.
Knight's Cross on January 9, 1945 as commander of the Parachute Mortar Instruction Battalion with the rank of Hauptmann.
Died on November 17, 1984 in Hemer, Märkisch District.

Milch joined the Reichswehr on April 1, 1924 and served as a volunteer in the 6th (Prussian) Artillery Regiment in Minden. Promoted to *Leutnant* on March 1, 1939, he went into the Second World War with the 603rd Motorized Special Purpose Artillery Regiment. He saw action in the eastern campaign from June 22, 1941 as battery officer and commander of the signals platoon. Milch won the Iron Cross, First Class and was promoted to *Oberleutnant* on October 31, 1941.

On December 17, 1941 Milch joined the 1st Parachute Regiment's 5th Battery as battery officer and saw action in the central sector of the Eastern Front.

Milch served in Africa with the Ramcke Brigade from August to November 1942. His battery, armed with 105mm light cannon, fought in a defensive role at Bab el Quattara and destroyed a number of enemy tanks and trucks.

Transferred to Italy with the 2nd Parachute Division, Milch took part in the Battle of Rome. In the winter of 1943 he returned to Russia with the 2nd Parachute Division, commanding II Battalion, 2nd Parachute Artillery Regiment in the defensive struggle there. He and his battery held Zhaikovka airfield and fought successfully at Juchnov.

In August 1944 Milch fought with the newly-formed mortar battalion with the 5th Parachute Division near Nancy and smashed the American bridgehead at Flavigny. Milch's actions were praised in an order of the day issued by the First Parachute Army. He was awarded the Knight's Cross.

Milch's last battle was fought at Bad Zwischenahn airport, where on May 5, 1945 he repulsed a heavy attack by enemy tanks.

GERD MISCHKE

Born on March 16, 1920 in Barmen, Wuppertal District.
Ultimate rank: Hauptmann.
Last service position: Commander of 4th Company, 2nd Parachute Anti-tank Battalion.
German Cross in Gold on January 1, 1945.
Knight's Cross on May 18, 1943 as company commander of 1st Company, 2nd Parachute Anti-tank Battalion with the rank of Leutnant.

Gerd Mischke joined the 82nd Flight Training Regiment in Osnabrück on April 14, 1939. After several postings he arrived at the 7th Flak Battalion's 2nd Battery on July 19, 1940. From there he joined the parachute troops as a *Gefreiter* and took the parachutist-rifleman course at Wittstock-Dosse. On December 15, 1940 he joined the 2nd Company of the Parachute Anti-aircraft Machine-gun Battalion in Aschersleben.

Mischke's first action was the jump into Crete, in which he took part as an *Unteroffizier*. Mischke fought as a gun commander in the Rethymnon area; on May 22 repulsed an enemy attack with his 20mm flak and led the subsequent counterattack. This won Mischke the Iron Cross, First Class.

In the winter battle on the Neva Mischke fought in the notorious Petrushino bridgehead, where he led another counterattack with his 20mm flak.

After returning from Russia Mischke served in the home war zone, defending against enemy bombers. On June 19, 1942 he was promoted to *Leutnant.*

With the establishment of the Tunis bridgehead Mischke saw action in Northwest Africa. He and several comrades stopped an advance by American tanks south of Mateur. During the attack by the von Manteuffel Division west from the Jefna position on March 7 and 8, 1943 Mischke and his unit provided the anti-tank defense. Mischke himself destroyed an enemy heavy tank from a distance of 40 meters. On May 5 his five 40mm anti-tank guns destroyed six enemy tanks and foiled an enemy breakthrough attempt. Mischke was awarded the Knight's Cross. In Fortress Brest he won the German Cross in Gold, which was awarded on January 1, 1945.

KARL NEUHOFF

Born on April 24, 1914 in Gevelsberg.
Ultimate rank: Oberleutnant.
Last service position: Commander of I Battalion, 3rd Parachute Regiment.
German Cross in Gold on October 27, 1943.
Knight's Cross on June 9, 1944 as an assault team leader in 6th Company, 3rd Parachute Regiment with the rank of Oberfeldwebel.

Karl Neuhoff joined III (Light Infantry) Battalion of the 17th Infantry Regiment on November 3, 1937 and after serving barely six months transferred to the parachute troops. He graduated from the parachutist-rifleman course in Stendal on July 15, 1939. On September 1, 1939 he became a squad leader in 10th Company, 17th Infantry regiment and saw action in the Polish Campaign. From June 4, 1940 he served as a squad leader in the 7th Fliegerdivision's Parachute Replacement Battalion. Neuhoff was promoted to *Feldwebel* on December 1, 1940.

On April 16, 1941 Neuhoff joined 7th Company, 3rd Parachute Regiment as a squad leader. He participated in the airborne invasion of Crete with this unit and won both Iron Crosses.

Neuhoff did two tours of duty in Russia. On October 12 he was wounded and subsequently received the Wound Badge in Black. A month later he was wounded a second time.

In the Battle of Sicily Neuhoff saw action in a defensive role in the Lentini area under the command of the Schmalz Brigade. He was one of the last soldiers to cross over to the mainland, on August 16, 1943. There his unit continued to serve in a defensive role. On October 27, 1943 Neuhoff received the German Cross in Gold.

Neuhoff's finest hour was during the fighting at Cassino. When New Zealand troops drove into Cassino city from the north on March 15, 1944 they were stopped by Neuhoff and his men. They fought and stopped the 26th New Zealand Battalion from the Hotel Continental, as well as the 24th Battalion which followed. This won Neuhoff the Knight's Cross. He was promoted to *Oberleutnant* on December 29, 1944 and led I Battalion, 3rd Parachute Regiment until the end of the war.

DR. HEINRICH NEUMANN

Born on February 17, 1908 in Berlin-Steglitz.
Ultimate rank: Oberstarzt.
Last service position: Oberstarzt and Corps Medical Officer of II Parachute Corps.
Knight's Cross on August 21, 1941 as an Oberstabsarzt and acting commander of I Battalion, 1st Parachute Assault Regiment.

Heinrich Neumann joined the 9th Infantry Regiment's 15th Company on January 2, 1933 and on June 1 of that year was assigned to the 6th (Prussian) First-aid Battalion. On March 29, 1934 he moved to the Luftwaffe and on June 18, 1934 graduated from the University of Münster as a doctor of medicine.

Neumann went to Berlin as an aviation station medical officer and on July 17, 1937 went to Staaken for flight training. On May 31, 1938 Neuhoff was promoted to *Stabsarzt*.

Following several postings and completion of parachute-rifle training in Stendal, on February 19, 1939 he joined the Luftwaffe First-aid Echelon in Frankfurt on the Oder and from there went to Magdeburg. Neumann joined the parachute troops as commander of the 7th Luftwaffe First-aid Company in Gardelegen. He became commanding officer of the 7th Parachute First-aid Battalion and on October 15, 1940 regimental medical officer of the 1st Parachute Assault Regiment.

Neumann took part in the battle at Wola Gulowska and the parachute assault on Fortress Holland, where he was decorated with the Iron Cross, First Class.

During the airborne invasion of Crete, Neumann assumed command of I Battalion after *Major* Koch was put out of action and stormed Hill 107, from which the enemy was firing on Malemes airfield. The subsequent attack saw him and his battalion participate in the eastward advance by the German forces. Neumann was awarded the Knight's Cross.

Neumann later served in Russia where he was able to rescue 5,000 wounded from the Juchnov pocket. On February 6, 1942 he was promoted to *Oberfeldarzt* and on September 1 to *Oberstarzt*. He served as division medical officer with the 6th Parachute Division and corps medical officer of II Parachute Corps until the end of the war.

HEINRICH ORTH

Born on January 4, 1916 in Herrensohr, Dudweiler District, Saar.
Ultimate rank: Leutnant.
Last service position: Platoon leader in 4th Company, 1st Parachute Regiment.
Knight's Cross on March 18, 1942.
Killed in action on March 10, 1942 near Zhaikovka.

Heinrich Orth joined the 1st Battery of the 4th Flak Regiment in Dortmund on October 1, 1935 and in 1938 volunteered for service with the parachute troops. He completed the parachutist-rifleman course on April 1, 1938 after which he was assigned to 1st Company, 1st Parachute Regiment.

As an *Oberjäger* and company squad leader, Orth showed in Poland that he was a fighter.

Orth fought bravely in the battles for the Belgian frontier fortress Eben Emael and the bridges over the Albert Canal. He freed two squads which had been surrounded by the enemy, one of which included the assault group commander, *Leutnant* Schacht, and won both Iron Crosses. Orth was promoted to *Feldwebel* for bravery in the face of the enemy.

On July 1, 1941 Orth was promoted to *Oberfeldwebel*. He took part in the bitter fighting in Russia in the fall and winter of 1941-42 as a platoon leader in 4th Company, 1st Parachute Assault Regiment. As a platoon leader Orth saw action in critical situations in Zhaikovska and Anisovo-Gorodische. In those weeks of uninterrupted fighting Orth became a symbol of courage and steadfastness. He led his platoon and occasionally also the company and drove the enemy out of the villages.

On March 10, 1942 Orth led his platoon into an enemy-occupied village near Zhaikovska. The enemy were driven out of the village but Orth was killed in this pitiless struggle.

Orth was buried in the German cemetery in Zhaikovska beside *Leutnant* Arpke. On March 18 it was announced that Orth had been awarded the Knight's Cross.

GERHARD PADE

Born on June 21, 1912 in Berlin.
Ultimate rank: Major.
Last service position: Commander of I Battalion, 4th Parachute Regiment.
German Cross in Gold on August 20, 1944.
Knight's Cross on April 30, 1945 as commander of I Battalion, 4th Parachute Regiment with the rank of Major.

Gerhard Pade entered the police service on October 1, 1932. He passed a series of training courses and on September 1, 1935 became a police *Wachtmeister.*

Pade reported to the parachute troops on May 24, 1937 and took part in the 6th parachutist-rifleman course at Stendal. On April 1, 1938 he joined I Battalion, 1st Parachute Regiment.

In January 1939 Pade successfully completed a senior NCO course. He was well known as an athlete and won a number of titles as a hammer thrower.

The Western Campaign saw Pade in action in Fortress Holland. There he won both Iron Crosses within a week and distinguished himself through daring attacks.

Pade again gave cause for much comment in Crete. On June 1, 1941 he was named a wartime officer candidate and following an officer course joined 2nd Company, 1st Parachute Regiment, commanded by *Oberleutnant* Zuber. Pade became a platoon leader and was a key element in the regiment's defensive actions in Russia, where he led 1st Company for a time.

From May 5, 1943 to January 3, 1944 Pade was commander of 14th (Anti-tank) Company, 1st Parachute Regiment and on January 28 he went to Versailles for a company commander course. On April 1, 1943 he was promoted to *Hauptmann.*

Pade won the German Cross in Gold in the Italian battle zone on August 20, 1944. He stood fast between Bologna and Imola in very heavy defensive fighting and from December 8, 1944 led I Battalion, 4th Parachute Regiment. He held the defensive positions and guarded the crossings of the Po and the Schio Rivers.

HUGO PAUL

Born on February 1, 1913 in Villingen, Giessen District.
Ultimate rank: Major.
Last service position: Commander of III Battalion, 21st Parachute Regiment.
Knight's Cross on November 18, 1944 as commander of Parachute Battalion "Paul" with the rank of Hauptmann.

Hugo Paul joined the 15th Regiment in Marburg-Lahn on April 20, 1931. He progressed from squad to company headquarters squad leader and finally platoon leader in the 15th and 115th Regiments. On April 1, 1937 Paul was assigned to the Hannover Cavalry School.

Paul received his promotion to *Feldwebel* on August 1, 1937. On June 1, 1940 he became an *Oberfeldwebel* and reported to Parachute School III, Braunschweig for parachute training. Soon afterward he became commander of 12th Company, 1st Parachute Assault Regiment.

After passing through the Luftwaffe Officer Candidate School in Berlin-Gatow Paul saw action in Crete. When his company commander was killed he took command of 4th Company, 1st Parachute Assault Regiment. He won both Iron Crosses and on September 1, 1941 was promoted to *Oberleutnant,* bypassing the rank of *Leutnant.* The same day he became the commanding officer of 4th Company, 1st Parachute Assault Regiment.

In Russia Paul saw action at Anisovo-Gorodische and in January 1942 was one of the most successful patrol leaders, inflicting serious defeats on the enemy. Paul received a personal letter of appreciation from *Generaloberst* von Richthofen.

After recovering from wounds suffered in combat Paul saw action in Tunisia. Serving with the 5th Parachute Division, he was company commander of 5th Company and ordnance officer in the Schirmer Battalion. Paul became ill and returned to Germany. He was promoted to *Hauptmann* on April 1, 1943 and served as an instructor. On April 1, 1944 he became commander of Parachute Battalion "Paul," with which he saw action near Overloon and Venlo. Several attacks by enemy tanks were repulsed and the enemy was driven out of Overloon. Paul received the Knight's Cross on November 28, 1944 and on February 1, 1945 was promoted to *Major.*

HERBERT PEITSCH

Born on May 1, 1922 in Berlin.
Ultimate rank: Gefreiter.
Last service position: Mortarman in 7th Company, 6th Parachute Regiment.
Knight's Cross on October 29, 1944 as a mortarman with the rank of Gefreiter.
Killed in action on August 26 (?), 1944 on the Western Front.

Herbert Peitsch joined the 205 Infantry Replacement Regiment's 5th Company on August 7, 1941 and fought with his division in the Russian campaign. There he won the Iron Cross, Second Class on April 17, 1943.

After his fourth application to the parachute troops Peitsch was transferred to the 6th Parachute Regiment, which had been formed by *Major* Friedrich-August von der Heydte in January 1944. When he joined the unit it had just been transferred to Normandy.

Peitsch was present when *General* Student visited the unit on June 5, 1944, the evening before the invasion in the west. From the next day on he was in action in the Carentan area. When American paratroops of the 101st Airborne Division were dropped during the night of June 6 it was Peitsch who rounded up scattered enemy groups and brought them in as prisoners. His battalion commander, *Hauptmann* Mager, recommended him for the Knight's Cross, especially since Peitsch had also knocked out a number of air-landed vehicles with mortar fire.

When the commander of 7th Company was killed *Feldwebel* Otto Neitzel took command. With only 28 men he led a successful breakout through enemy lines.

The enemy advance was halted in the Battle of Ste. Mère Eglise. German forces were pinned down at Carentan and there was bitter fighting. *Major* Mager rejected a demand that the paratroops surrender.

Peitsch was a tower of strength in the fighting at Coutances and Poncey and especially at Vire. He was killed on August 6 or 7 while defending against an American attack.

ERICH PIETZONKA

Born on October 4, 1906 in Plümkenau, Silesia.
Ultimate rank: Oberst.
Last service position: Commander of the 7th Parachute Regiment in Fortress Brest.
German Cross in Gold on August 4, 1942.
Knight's Cross on September 5, 1944 as commander of the 7th Parachute Regiment with the rank of Oberstleutnant.
Oak Leaves (584th recipient) on September 16, 1944 as commander of the 7th Parachute Regiment in Fortress Brest with the rank of Oberst.
Deceased, date unknown.

Erich Pietzonka joined the 14th Company of the 7th Prussian Infantry Regiment in Schweidnitz, Silesia on November 1, 1924. On December 1, 1933 he was promoted to *Oberfeldwebel* at the Jüterbog Technical School. After completing the officer course at Hildesheim Flying School and other courses, the last at Tutow Flying School, on April 1, 1936 he was promoted to *Hauptmann*.

Pietzonka served with the Condor Legion as Chief-of-Staff in 1937. Later he was commander of the 1st Company of the Luftwaffe Guard Battalion in Berlin. On September 1, 1939 he became commander of 9th Company, General Göring Regiment.

Following parachute training, on July 15, 1940 Pietzonka was made commander of II Battalion, 2nd Parachute Regiment. On April 26, 1941 he participated in the parachute operation against the Corinth Canal as a Major with the 2nd Parachute Regiment commanded by *Oberst* Sturm. Pietzonka sustained serious injuries on landing.

Pietzonka rejoined II Battalion, 2nd Parachute Regiment and was present during the defensive actions at the Volkhov and the Mius in 1942-43, winning the German Cross in Gold there.

On June 26, 1943 Pietzonka was placed in command of the 2nd Parachute Regiment and led the unit during the German occupation of Rome.

During the winter of 1943 Pietzonka and his regiment battled the attacking Russians at Zhitomir and Kirovograd. He subsequently saw action in Normandy and finally in Fortress Brest, where he was taken prisoner by American forces on September 19, 1944.

Fritz Prager

Born on December 17, 1905 in Wolfenbüttel, Lower Saxony.
Ultimate rank: Major.
Last service position: Commander of III Battalion, 3rd Parachute Regiment.
Knight's Cross on May 24, 1940.
Died on December 3, 1940.

Fritz Prager joined the Reichswehr on November 26, 1923 as a member of the 10th (Saxon) Infantry Regiment. He was promoted to *Leutnant* on June 1, 1930, *Oberleutnant* on July 1, 1933 and *Hauptmann* on April 1, 1937.

On July 12, 1938 he joined the parachute troops as a volunteer and completed the parachutist-rifleman course in Stendal. On January 1, 1939 he became commanding officer of II Battalion, 1st Parachute Regiment in Braunschweig.

Prager's battalion was one of the few parachute units to see action in Poland, where it captured Wola Gulowska airfield. On October 13, 1939 Prager was decorated with the Iron Cross, Second Class by *General* Student.

On April 30, 1940 Prager underwent an inguinal operation, but this did not keep him from jumping with his battalion over Holland. He led his troops in the storming of Moerdijk Bridge. Prager was badly wounded taking a number of stout enemy bunkers. He remained with the battalion, which held the bridge until relieved by tanks of the 9th Panzer Division. Prager had already won the Iron Cross, First Class on May 10, and this was followed by the Knight's Cross on May 24, 1940.

When Prager learned that his battalion was to be deployed to relieve the mountain infantry near Narvik nothing could keep him in hospital. He took part in this operation as well.

Prager was promoted to Major on June 19, 1940 and on July 1 took command of the 3rd Parachute Regiment's II Battalion. He died on December 3, 1940.

BERNHARD HERMANN RAMCKE

Born on January 24, 1889.
Ultimate rank: General der Fallschirmtruppe.
Last service position: Military commander of Fortress Brest.
Imperial Prussian Distinguished Service Cross on April 20, 1918.
Wound Badge in Gold on November 3, 1919.
Knight's Cross on August 21, 1941 as commander of the 1st Parachute Assault Regiment in Crete.
Oak Leaves (145th recipient) on November 13, 1942 as commander of the Ramcke Brigade in Africa.
Swords (99th recipient) on September 19, 1944 as commander of Fortress Brest.
Diamonds (20th recipient) on September 19, 1944 as commander of Fortress Brest.
Died on July 4, 1968 in Kappeln, Schleswig.

Ramcke joined the Imperial Navy on April 4, 1905 as a cabin boy on the SMS *Stosch*. He distinguished himself as a member of the Marine Assault Battalion Flanders and was promoted to *Leutnant* on July 18, 1918.

Ramcke transferred to the army on March 10, 1919, fought with the Freikorps Brandis in Upper Silesia and was subsequently taken into the Reichswehr. On February 1, 1927 Ramcke was promoted to *Hauptmann* and served as commander of the 11th Company of the 2nd Prussian Infantry Regiment. Following a series of appointments he was promoted to *Major* on September 1, 1934 and commanded a battalion of the 3rd Infantry Division.

Ramcke became an *Oberstleutnant* on March 16, 1937 and on July 19, 1940 was transferred (at his request) to the 7th Air Division. He joined the parachute troops on July 31, 1940 and earned the parachutist-rifleman badge at the age of fifty-one.

As an *Oberst* Ramcke won the Knight's Cross during the campaign on Crete. In the summer of 1942 he oversaw the formation of the Italian Folgore Parachute Division. Ramcke subsequently commanded the Ramcke Parachute Brigade, which caused a sensation in North Africa, where he won the Oak Leaves.

On February 13, 1943 Ramcke was named commanding officer of the 2nd Parachute Division, which he led in the east and west. In the fortress of Brest Ramcke and his division held out until September 19, 1944 against a tenfold enemy superiority. There he won the Swords and the Diamonds.

SIEGFRIED RAMMELT

Born on December 18, 1914 in Falkenberg, Herzberg District.
Ultimate rank: Oberleutnant.
Last service position: Leader of the Regimental Pioneer Platoon, 3rd Parachute Regiment.
German Cross in Gold on February 5, 1944.
Knight's Cross on June 9, 1944 as leader of an assault team near Monte Cassino.
Killed in action on March 21, 1944 near Cassino.

After completing his period of work with the labor service, on November 1, 1935 Rammelt joined the 32nd Infantry Regiment's 6th Company in Eilenburg. On October 4, 1937, then an *Unteroffizier* and reserve officer candidate, he was released to work as an aviation electrician with the Junkers works in Dessau. He successfully passed the engineering school in Weimar in a year, and on May 25, 1938 took part in his first reserve exercise with his old regiment. A second exercise followed, and on May 25, 1938 Rammelt was promoted to *Feldwebel*.

Called up by the 81st Infantry Regiment on October 11, 1939, Rammelt volunteered for the parachute troops and completed the parachutist-rifleman course in Stendal. On July 25, 1940 he joined 11th Company, 3rd Parachute Regiment then passed an officer candidate course in Braunschweig as well as two other courses.

Rammelt took part in the airborne invasion of Crete as a member of the 3rd Parachute Regiment's 11th Company. He participated in the bitter fighting for possession of the island and won both Iron Crosses. On August 30, 1941 Rammelt completed training as a platoon leader in Döberitz.

On October 23, 1941, during the early stages of the Russian Campaign, Rammelt was seriously wounded during the bitter fighting at the Neva River.

Considered officer material by the regimental command, Rammelt was sent for further training, which concluded at the Luftwaffe School of Warfare at Gross-Born. On April 20, 1943 he was promoted to *Oberleutnant*.

Rammelt distinguished himself repeatedly during the Battle of Monte Cassino. He successfully led the most difficult offensive patrols and was decorated with the Knight's Cross, but not until several months after his death.

ERNST WILLI RAPRÄGER

Born on September 15, 1918 in Strasbourg, Alsace.
Ultimate rank: Major.
Last service position: Commander of the 21st Parachute Rocket Battalion.
Knight's Cross on May 10, 1943 as commander of a battle group in the Luftwaffe Barenthin Regiment in Africa with the rank of Oberleutnant.

Ernst Willi Rapräger joined the 4th Battery of the 12th Flak Regiment in Berlin after completing his period of service with the Reich Labor Service. He served with the flak arm and when war broke out his unit was stationed in the Westwall.

Promoted to *Leutnant* on February 1, 1940, on July 1 Rapräger joined the parachute troops and completed the parachutist-rifleman course at Parachute School III in Braunschweig.

Rapräger served as a platoon leader in various companies and on April 1, 1942 received his promotion to *Oberleutnant.* On May 19, 1942 he was transferred to the officer reserve of IV Battalion, 1st Parachute Regiment.

Following a transfer to the Rocket Batteries Testing Battalion, part of the Parachute Instruction Regiment, on October 28, 1942 he became commander of 15th Battery, 1st Parachute Artillery Regiment.

When, in response to the allied landings in Northwest Africa the Luftwaffe's Barenthin Regiment, commanded by the officer in charge of the corps units of XI Fliegerkorps, *Oberst* Barenthin, was sent to Africa, Willi Rapräger served as commander of a battle group in the regiment's III Battalion. He successfully repelled several powerful enemy attacks in the northern sector of the Tunisian theater. Rapräger was awarded the Knight's Cross for his iron steadfastness and on May 10, 1944 was promoted to *Hauptmann.*

On July 15, 1944 Rapräger took over the 21st Parachute Rocket Battalion south of Nimwegen, where on September 17 he repulsed several strong attacks by American forces. Rapräger was severely wounded while personally leading an offensive patrol near Riethorst on September 17, 1944.

ADOLF REININGHAUS

Born on December 6, 1915 in Remschneid.
Ultimate rank: Oberfeldwebel.
Last service position: Platoon leader in the 14th Company, 7th Parachute Regiment.
Knight's Cross on September 13, 1944 as a platoon leader in Fortress Brest with the rank of Oberfeldwebel.

Reininghaus joined the Luftwaffe on November 1, 1936. On August 17, 1937 he completed an NCO course and on October 1 was promoted to *Gefreiter.* Exactly a year later he became an *Obergefreiter.*

Reininghaus joined the 1st Parachute Regiment on January 1, 1940 and after completing parachute training was promoted to *Oberjäger* on May 1, 1940.

Reininghaus won the Iron Cross, Second Class in the Balkans on March 17, 1941. The campaign against Russia saw him in action in the northern sector of the Eastern Front, where he was decorated with the Iron Cross, First Class on December 18, 1941. On April 1 of the following year he was promoted to *Feldwebel.*

In 1943 Reininghaus joined the 7th Parachute Regiment of the 2nd Parachute Division. There he received a promotion to *Oberfeldwebel* on February 5, 1944.

Reininghaus saw action during the Battle of Normandy as a member of the 7th Parachute Regiment. When allied forces broke through near Avranches, the 2nd Parachute Division under *Generalleutnant* Ramcke was sent to the western theater. As part of the division's movements, the 7th Parachute Regiment under *Oberst* Pietzonka moved up the Sizun road into the Commana, where it halted the Americans, and into the Hueloat area. There it fought a three-day battle with American armored units. 32 enemy tanks were destroyed. The 2nd Parachute Division reached Fortress Brest. That it hadn't already been encircled and wiped out was due to the 7th Parachute Regiment and Reininghaus, who was awarded the Knight's Cross on September 3, 1944. Adolf Reininghaus was taken prisoner by the Americans on September 19, 1944 and was released in 1947.

PAUL-ERNST RENISCH

Born on July 2, 1917 in Brussels, Belgium.
Ultimate rank: Major.
Last service position: Commander of I Battalion, 1st Parachute Regiment.
German Cross in Gold on April 22, 1944.
Knight's Cross on October 31, 1944 as commander of I Battalion, 1st Parachute Regiment with the rank of Hauptmann.

Renisch joined the flak arm on November 2, 1936 in Dessau, home of the 26th Flak Regiment. He became a *Leutnant* on December 1, 1938 and joined the 340th Motorized Searchlight Battalion as signals officer. On October 1, 1941 Renisch joined the parachute troops, where he was promoted to *Oberleutnant* on December 1, 1941. From the Parachute Instruction Battalion Berlin he went to 2nd Company, 1st Parachute Regiment. Renisch was placed in charge of the company and later made company commander. In autumn 1942 Renisch and 2nd Company were sent to Russia.

Renisch led 2nd Company in the bitter winter fighting in the Orel bend and participated in the recapture of the village of Stonotishe and the defense of Hills 266 and 262.3. He and his men held out against heavy Russian attacks and Renisch was awarded the Iron Cross, First Class. On January 28, 1943 Renisch took command of I Battalion, 1st Parachute Regiment after the battalion commander was wounded and on April 4 was named company commander of 1st Parachute Regiment's 9th Company.

Renisch achieved two major defensive successes near Ortona during the fighting on the Italian mainland. In the second battle of Cassino he was awarded the German Cross in Gold for a series of heroic actions.

Promoted to *Hauptmann* on June 21, 1944, that summer Renisch took part in the heavy fighting on the Adriatic at Pesaro, Cattolica and Rimini. There he commanded III Battalion, 1st Parachute Regiment, which frustrated every outflanking attempt by the enemy. This won Renisch the Knight's Cross.

On March 1, 1945 Renisch was promoted to *Major;* he was captured by the British on May 2, 1945 during the German retreat.

RUDOLF RENNECKE

Born on June 19, 1915 in Leipzig.
Ultimate rank: Oberstleutnant.
Last service position: Commander of the 1st Parachute Regiment.
German Cross in Gold on December 12, 1943.
Knight's Cross on June 9, 1944 as commander of II Battalion, 3rd Parachute Regiment with the rank of Hauptmann.
Oak Leaves (664th recipient) on November 25, 1944 as commander of the 1st Parachute Regiment with the rank of Major.
Died on March 3, 1986 in Bayerisch Gmain.

Rennecke joined the 32nd Infantry Regiment's 13th Company in Grimma on November 2, 1937 and on August 27, 1938 reported for the army's 7th parachutist-rifleman course. He was transferred to the Parachute Infantry Battalion under the command of *Major* Heidrich and completed junior NCO and combat engineer courses.

As an *Oberjäger* Rennecke took part in the German parachute troops' first battle at Wola Gulowska airfield. In May 1940, as a *Feldwebel*, he parachuted into Fortress Holland near the Moerdijk bridges. There he eliminated a machine-gun nest and took a number of prisoners while storming a farm with only two companions.

Rennecke received the Iron Cross, First Class on May 16, 1940 and on July 11 was promoted to *Leutnant* for bravery in the face of the enemy.

Following the Crete operation Rennecke fought in the northern sector of the Eastern Front, where he was badly wounded on November 4, 1941.

Rennecke served as regimental adjutant of the 3rd Parachute Regiment for more than a year before taking command of the 3rd Parachute Regiment's II Battalion near Ortona. Later he was named military commander of Cassino city. He and his battalion defended the city, which resulted in Rennecke receiving the Knight's Cross. On June 5, 1944 he was promoted to *Major* and named special duties officer of the 3rd Parachute Regiment. Rennecke was placed in command of the 1st Parachute Regiment on June 20, 1944. He and his regiment fought a bitter defensive battle in the Rimini area and near Bologna. Rennecke was awarded the Oak Leaves. He led his regiment until the end of the war.

HELMUT RINGLER

Born on October 4, 1915 in Wollstein, Witzenhausen District.
Ultimate rank: Hauptmann.
Last service position: Commander of II Battalion, 2nd Parachute Regiment.
Knight's Cross on May 15, 1940 as leader of an heavy machine-gun demi-platoon in the "Stahl" Airborne Group with the rank of Leutnant.

When Helmut Ringler joined the 9th Flak regiment in Münster on November 4, 1935, he had no way of knowing that he would some day join the parachute troops. This took place on September 26, 1939, the day of official mobilization. He was assigned to the Koch Parachute Assault Battalion, where on April 1, 1940 he became a platoon leader in 4th Company.

Ringler parachuted into Fortress Holland with his platoon. Assigned to the "Stahl" Assault Group under *Oberleutnant* Altmann, whose objective was the capture of the Veldwezelt Bridge over the Albert Canal, he and his demi-platoon jumped in the second wave at 06.15 hours to reinforce the assault group, which was in the midst of heavy fighting.

He and his men landed under heavy fire. Ringler immediately assembled the men and overpowered the enemy troops manning a section of trench directly in front of them. He found two weapons containers, after which he was able to eliminate the enemy with strong flanking fire and relieve the pressure on the hard-pressed assault group. *Leutnant* Ringler distinguished himself through his extraordinary bravery. He turned up wherever the situation was in doubt and held the captured positions against all enemy attacks until army units arrived to relieve the paratroops.

Ringler received both Iron Crosses on May 12 and 13 and the Knight's Cross on May 14. On May 20 he was promoted to *Leutnant* for bravery in the face of the enemy.

As a result of wounds suffered in Holland Ringler was no longer fit for combat and subsequently served in the parachute officer reserve. He became commander of a training company in Stendal and served in other posts in Germany. Ringler finally returned to action as commander of II Battalion, 2nd Parachute Regiment in the west.

ARNOLD VON ROON

Born on July 19, 1914 in Berlin-Friedenau.
Ultimate rank: General Staff Major.
Last service position: Ia of the First Parachute Army.
Spanish Cross in Gold with Swords on June 6, 1939.
Knight's Cross on July 9, 1941 as commander of 3rd Company, 2nd Parachute Regiment with the rank of Oberleutnant.
Deceased (date unknown).

Arnold von Roon joined the German Armed Forces on April 1, 1934. He was assigned to the 3rd Cavalry Regiment in Rathenow, part of the 1st Cavalry Division. On January 1, 1935 he transferred to the Luftwaffe, completed flight training and joined Fliegergruppe Prenzlau. On April 20, 1936 he became a *Leutnant* and subsequently served as an observer with A/88, the long-range reconnaissance Staffel of the Condor Legion. Von Roon was decorated three times in Spain.

Promoted to *Oberleutnant* on October 30, 1938, von Roon served as operations officer in the Ia section of the 7th Air Division. From there he reported to the parachute troops and completed the parachutist-rifleman course in Stendal by March 24, 1939. On April 1, 1940 he became company commander of 3rd Company, 2nd Parachute Regiment and saw action with this unit in Holland. With the exception of the Genz Platoon, his company was dropped in the wrong place. Nevertheless von Roon managed to reach the headquarters of the 22nd Airborne (Glider) Division via Monster. Von Roon won both Iron Crosses in the fighting in Holland.

The campaign in the Balkans saw him in action at the Corinth Canal. Von Roon jumped in the second wave at Crete; he and his company landed seven kilometers west of their objective, Rethymnon airfield. Von Roon took a vineyard hill, fought his way through to the center of Rethymnon airfield and finally, on May 27, captured the enemy-occupied Hill 156. Von Roon received the Knight's Cross for his actions on Crete.

On September 19, 1941 von Roon was promoted to *Hauptmann*. He served in staff positions until the end of the war and received a promotion to *Major* on February 25, 1945.

WALTER SANDER

Born on July 25, 1914 in Völksen an der Deister, Lower Saxony.
Ultimate rank: Oberleutnant.
Last service position: Commander of 1st Company, 5th Parachute Pioneer Battalion.
German Cross in Gold on February 8, 1943.
Knight's Cross on February 28, 1945.
Died on April 28, 1981 in Springe an der Deister, Lower Saxony.

Walter Sander joined the Wehrmacht on October 1, 1935. He served until October 7, 1937 and left the armed forces with the rank of *Unteroffizier.* On August 30, 1939 Sander returned, joining the 4th Company of the Parachute Pioneer Battalion.

His first parachute action was Crete. Sander won both Iron Crosses there and on October 1, 1941 was promoted to *Feldwebel.*

Sander was badly wounded on the Neva front in northern Russia on October 30, 1941. In spite of this he was present during the battalion's second tour of duty in Russia. During the bitter fighting in the Lake Ilmen area from October 28, 1942 to January 13, 1941 Sander proved himself while leading offensive patrols. A dozen such operations earned him the German Cross in Gold.

On April 7, 1943 he was sent as a wartime officer candidate to Dessau-Rosslau (pioneer) for an officer course. Sander subsequently parachuted into Sicily. On January 1, 1944, now stationed on the Italian mainland, he was promoted to *Leutnant.*

In Normandy Sander led the 5th Parachute Pioneer Battalion's 4th Company. The company held its sector for 16 days against heavy enemy attacks.

Sander also distinguished himself in the Ardennes offensive, where he fought alongside the 11th Parachute Assault Gun Brigade. Together they drove deep into the enemy rear and captured a signals battalion of the American 28th Division. Sander took another 200 prisoners in Wiltz. On December 18, 1944 he was promoted to *Oberleutnant* and on February 29, 1945 received the Knight's Cross.

BRUNO SASSEN

Born on March 13, 1918 in Mittermoor, Leer District, Ostfriesland.
Ultimate rank: Leutnant.
Last service position: Officer with Leer Station Headquarters.
German Cross in Gold on August 2, 1943.
Knight's Cross on February 22, 1942 as a squad leader in 10th Company, 3rd Parachute Regiment with the rank of Feldwebel.

Bruno Sassen joined the 13th Cavalry Regiment's 2nd Squadron in Lüneburg on November 4, 1937. On October 1, 1938 he became a reserve veterinary officer candidate and was sent to the army's veterinary academy in Hannover. Sassen began his studies in veterinary medicine in Hannover on April 1, 1939. On September 27, 1939 he was recalled to active service.

Sassen reported to the parachute troops on June 1, 1940; after completing parachute training he was assigned to 10th Company, 3rd Parachute Regiment. He was to stay with this company until March 27, 1943.

Now an *Oberjäger*, Sassen saw action in Crete southwest of Chania. He and 30 men stormed a British tent camp. Sassen was wounded and taken prisoner, but was freed seven days later. He received both Iron Crosses for his actions on Crete.

On October 1, 1941, his unit now at the Neva River in Russia, Sassen was promoted to *Feldwebel*. Daily he and his company repulsed enemy attacks on German positions in the Vyborgskaya bridgehead. Sassen and his two machine-guns halted the enemy there for 33 days. When the Russians captured the anti-tank ditch in front of his position on November 15, 1941, he and five comrades counterattacked and drove them out again. Sassen was awarded the Knight's Cross.

Sassen was badly wounded on March 27, 1943 while storming a vital hill during the fighting east of Twerdy in the central sector of the Eastern Front. He was decorated with the German Cross in Gold. Sassen did not return to combat. He was given a training command and shortly before the end of the war became special duties officer on the staff of the Leer Station Commander.

GERHARD SCHACHT

Born on April 6, 1916 in Berlin-Steglitz.
Ultimate rank: General Staff Major.
Last service position: Commander of the Special Purpose Parachute Regiment (later the 25th Parachute Regiment).
German Cross in Gold on December 21, 1944.
Knight's Cross on May 12, 1940 as a platoon leader in the "Beton" Assault Group with the rank of Leutnant.
Died on February 7, 1972 in Dortmund.

Gerhard Schacht joined the Reichswehr on November 1, 1934. He served for eleven months with the 3rd Motorized Reconnaissance Battalion in Wünsdorf before leaving the army with the rank of *Gefreiter*. Schacht returned to his old battalion on November 2, 1936 as a *Fahnenjunker-Gefreiter*. A course at the Dresden Officer Candidate School followed, before he transferred to the Luftwaffe on October 1, 1937. Schacht became a *Leutnant* on January 1, 1938.

On January 1, 1940 Koch was assigned to the "Friedrichshafen Test Battalion" (cover name for the Koch Assault Battalion). In the Western Campaign he was to lead Assault Group "Beton," whose objective was to seize and hold the Vroenhaven Bridge over the Albert Canal.

This assault group was dropped at 05.15 hours on May 10, 1940. *Gefreiter* Stenzel prevented the bridge from being blown. The enemy troops guarding the bridge were overpowered and 300 prisoners were taken. The assault group had fulfilled its mission.

Gerhard Schacht received both Iron Crosses and the Knight's Cross and was promoted to *Oberleutnant* on May 16, 1940.

Schacht was an operations officer with XI Fliegerkorps during the Crete operation. He was promoted to *Hauptmann* on February 25, 1942 and that summer became Ia of the Ramcke Parachute Brigade in Africa.

Schacht went to the Air Warfare Academy at Berlin-Gatow on April 10, 1943 and subsequently served in various staff positions.

MARTIN SCHÄCHTER

Born on March 14, 1915 in Petershagen, Minden District.
Ultimate rank: Major.
Last service position: Ib of the 3rd Parachute Division in the Ruhr Pocket.
Knight's Cross on May 12, 1940 as commander of Assault Group "Eisen" with the rank of Leutnant.

Martin Schächter joined the 18th Pioneer Battalion in Glogau, Silesia as a *Fahnenjunker* on April 1, 1935. One year later he was transferred to the Luftwaffe, where he was trained as a bomber observer. Schächter served in various posts with KG 152 and KG 53 and on January 1, 1938 was promoted to *Leutnant*.

Schächter subsequently joined the parachute troops and on January 1, 1939 became company officer in the 1st Parachute Regiment. On March 1, 1940 he was assigned to the Koch Assault Battalion, where he was placed in charge of the pioneer company.

On May 10, 1940 Schächter led Assault Group "Eisen" against the bridge over the Albert Canal at Canne. The group landed in ten gliders some time after the landings by the other groups and found that the enemy had already blown the bridge.

While mopping up the enemy trenches near the group's landing site Schächter was badly wounded in the head and leg, which resulted in nine months in hospital. In spite of this his assault group was victorious at Canne. *Leutnant* Meissner assumed command and held the bridgehead against heavy enemy attacks.

Just recovered from his wounds, Schächter, who had been promoted to *Oberleutnant* on May 16, 1940, parachuted into Crete as *General* Meindl's ordnance officer. He and his commanding officer were both badly wounded in the operation.

No longer fit for combat, Schächter served as an officer on the staff of the State Secretary of Aviation and *General* Inspector of the Luftwaffe, *Generalfeldmarschall* Milch. He later served on the staff of the 3rd Parachute Regiment and XI Fliegerkorps. On March 15, 1945 he was captured while serving as Ib of the 3rd Parachute Division in the Ruhr Pocket.

DIPL. ING. RICHARD SCHIMPF

Born on May 16, 1897 in Eggenfeld, Bavaria.
Ultimate rank: Generalleutnant.
Last service position: Commander of the 3rd Parachute Division.
German Cross in Gold on August 26, 1944.
Knight's Cross on October 6, 1944 as commander of the 3rd Parachute Division with the rank of Generalleutnant.
Died on December 30, 1972 in Düsseldorf.

On February 11, 1915 Rudolf Schimpf joined the 9th Royal Bavarian Infantry Regiment Wrede as a *Fahnenjunker*. During the First World War he fought on the Western Front as a platoon leader. After the war he was taken on strength by the 45th Reichswehr Regiment, Marienburg and on October 1, 1919 became a *Leutnant*.

After training as a pilot in April 1925, that autumn he began training as a command assistant (General Staff). He served in various positions and divisions and on October 1, 1930 began studying at the Berlin Technical High School. Schimpf passed his exams for a diploma of engineering on January 31, 1935.

Schimpf transferred to the Luftwaffe on March 1, 1935, became a *Staffelkapitän* and on April 1 was promoted to *Major*. After becoming an *Oberstleutnant* on April 1, 1937, on September 1, 1938 Schimpf joined the Luftwaffe General Staff. On October 1, 1939 he became a General Staff *Oberst* and as such took part in the campaign against France as Ia in the staff of the Luftwaffe general with Army Group A. Schimpf received the Knight's Cross on February 17, 1941.

On December 1, 1941 Schimpf was made head of the Kiev Air District after which he was named Chief-of-Staff of the Kharkov Air District. On September 29, 1942 he was given command of the "Meindl" Luftwaffe Division and soon afterward became commanding officer of the 21st Luftwaffe Field Division.

Promoted to *Generalmajor* on August 1, 1943, on February 17, 1944 he assumed command of the 3rd Parachute Division. On March 23, 1944 he was promoted to *Generalleutnant*. On March 8, 1945 he and his division were taken prisoner by the Americans near Bad Godesberg. Schimpf was released on December 22, 1947.

HORST SCHIMPKE

Born on November 10, 1920 in Berlin-Schöneberg.
Ultimate rank: Leutnant.
Last service position: Commander of 1st Company, 1st Parachute Anti-tank Battalion.
Knight's Cross on September 5, 1944 as commander of 1st Company, 1st Parachute Anti-tank Battalion with the rank of Leutnant.
Died on March 6, 1980, location unknown.

Schimpke found his first home in the military when he joined the 206th Anti-tank Company in Allenstein on September 3, 1939. After volunteering for the parachute troops, he began parachute training on August 16, 1940, beginning with the parachutist-rifleman course in Braunschweig.

Schimpke was subsequently transferred to the 3rd Company of the Parachute Anti-tank Battalion, part of the 7th Air Division, where he became a gun commander, then a platoon leader and deputy company commander.

His first action was at Crete, where he distinguished himself in 7th Company, 1st Parachute Anti-tank Battalion's battle for the vitally-important airfield at Malemes. *Obergefreiter* Schimpke received both Iron Crosses for his actions and was wounded for the first time.

Promoted to *Oberjäger* on October 1, 1940, Schimpke took part in the battles fought by the German Africa Corps, in particular Rommel's advance on January 21, 1942. He advanced with the Africa Corps as far as the east end of Cyrenaica. Then his unit was pulled out of Africa and transported to the central sector of the Eastern Front.

In July and August 1943 Schimpke saw action with his unit on Sicily. On April 1, 1943 he had been promoted to *Oberfeldwebel* and named a wartime officer candidate. Schimpke was promoted to *Leutnant* on August 1, 1943 while serving on the island of Sicily.

During the Third Battle of Cassino Horst Schimpke and his 1st Company were permanently on the defensive. By May 17, 1944 he had knocked out over 20 enemy tanks and repulsed several enemy attacks. This won him the Knight's Cross.

In the final phase of the Second World War Schimpke was placed in command of the 10th Parachute Anti-tank Battalion, which he led from March 1945 until the end of the war.

GERHART SCHIRMER

Born on January 9, 1913 in Chemnitz.
Ultimate rank: Oberstleutnant.
Last service position: Ia of the Parachute Training Division.
German Cross in Gold on June 13, 1943.
Knight's Cross on June 14, 1941 as commander of 6th Company, 2nd Parachute Regiment with the rank of Hauptmann.
Oak Leaves (657th recipient) on November 18, 1944 as commander of the 16th Parachute Regiment/East with the rank of Oberstleutnant.

After entering the Saxony State Police School on April 6, 1932 Schirmer passed through various police officer schools. On September 1, 1935 he transferred to the Luftwaffe and attended Oberschleissheim Pilot Training School. He moved to the parachute troops on May 1, 1939 and on September 15 became commander of 6th Company, 2nd Parachute Regiment in Tangermünde, later in Stendal.

Schirmer and his company took part in the parachute operation at the Corinth Canal and occupied the airfield there. After *Hauptmann* Pietzonka was injured while landing, Schirmer took command of II Battalion, 2nd Parachute Regiment and pursued the enemy across the Peloponnese, taking prisoner 72 British officers and 1,200 soldiers. 9,000 Greek troops, including the Commander-in-Chief of the army on the Peloponnese, also surrendered to him.

Hauptmann Schirmer landed near Heraklion as commander of the strategic reserve in the Crete operation. He captured Hill 296, for which he was awarded the Knight's Cross.

In the Tunisian area Schirmer initially led the 5th Parachute Regiment's III Battalion in the heavy defensive fighting and later assumed command of the regiment after *Oberstleutnant* Koch was put out of action.

On January 1, 1944 Schirmer became commanding officer of the 16th Parachute Regiment/East, with which he enjoyed great success in the East during the retreat into the positions guarding East Prussia and in the Memel bridgehead. He and his regiment were named in the Wehrmacht communique and the honor roll of the German Army.

On May 8, 1945 Schirmer was taken prisoner by the Soviets. It would be almost eleven years before he was released.

ALFRED SCHLEMM

Born on December 18, 1894 in Rudolstadt, Gera District, Thuringia.
Ultimate rank: General der Fallschirmtruppe.
Last service position: Acting Commander-in-Chief of the First Parachute Army.
German Cross in Gold on June 25, 1942.
Knight's Cross on June 11, 1944 as commanding general of the I Parachute Corps with the rank of General der Flieger.
Died on January 24, 1986 in Ahlten, near Hannover.

Alfred Schlemm joined the Prussian Army on March 8, 1913. On June 18, 1914 he went to the Danzig Officer Candidate School. Schlemm served in the First World War with the 56th Field Artillery Regiment, Posen as a platoon leader, operations officer, battery leader, battery commander and regimental adjutant. He won both Iron Crosses. After the war Schlemm fought with the forces protecting Germany's eastern frontier (Grenzschutz Ost).

Schlemm held various positions in the Reichswehr. On June 1, 1925 he was promoted to *Hauptmann*. It was to be another eleven years before he became a *Major*.

Assigned to the Wehrmacht Academy and subsequently to the RLM, Schlemm became an *Oberst* on February 1, 1938. He left the army and became Chief-of-Staff in the command of Air Defense Zone West.

Following further staff positions he became commander of the Luftwaffe Combat Unit Schlemm, part of VIII Fliegerkorps, and won the German Cross in Gold. On July 4, 1942 he was named commander of the 1st Air Division. Schlemm was promoted to *Generalleutnant* on June 1, 1942 and became commanding general of the II Luftwaffe Field Corps.

Schlemm was named commanding general of the I Parachute Corps on January 1, 1944 and fought with the unit in Italy. Named in the Wehrmacht communique, he received the Knight's Cross near Velletri. In the west Schlemm fought to the end with the First Parachute Army. He was wounded near Erle in Westphalia and was captured.

HERBERT SCHMIDT

Born on October 3, 1912 in Courbiére Fortress in Graudenz, Prussia.
Ultimate rank: Major.
Last service position: Ia of the 2nd Parachute Regiment.
Knight's Cross on May 29, 1940 as company commander of 1st Company, 1st Parachute Regiment with the rank of Oberleutnant.
Killed on June 16, 1944 near Pontivy, France.

Herbert Schmidt entered the Brandenburg-Havel Police School as a police officer candidate on April 6, 1932. On April 1, 1933 he joined the recently-formed Police Battalion Wecke, from which a short time later evolved the General Göring State Police Group. Schmidt completed the parachutist-rifleman course at Stendal on March 16, 1937 and on April 20 of that year became a *Leutnant* and company officer in IV (Parachute-Rifle) Battalion of the General Göring Regiment, which was incorporated into the parachute troops as I Battalion, 1st Parachute Regiment.

Schmidt became an Oberleutnant on October 1, 1939 and led 1st Company, 1st Parachute Regiment in Operation Weserübung. The company was dropped into Norway on the evening of April 14, 1940. Landing eight kilometers south of Dombas, for five days it prevented the British 148th Infantry Brigade from linking up with Norwegian forces. Schmidt and his 38 surviving men were taken prisoner by the Norwegians but were soon freed. Schmidt was awarded the Knight's Cross for this tremendous action.

On September 25, 1940, still not recovered from his wounds, Schmidt joined the staff of the Inspector-General of the Luftwaffe, *Generalfeldmarschall* Milch. He later became Ia of the 1st Luftwaffe Field Division and the 2nd Parachute Division.

On June 6, 1944, while driving from Vannes to Pontivy in Brittany, *Major* Herbert Schmidt was shot from behind by a French sniper while sitting beside his division commander, Bernhard Hermann Ramcke. He was killed instantly.

LEONHARD SCHMIDT

Born on December 9, 1916 in Weissenstadt, Upper Franconia.
Ultimate rank: Hauptmann.
Last service position: Commander of II Battalion, 1st Parachute Regiment.
German Cross in Gold on June 24, 1943.
Knight's Cross on April 30, 1945 as commander of II Battalion, 1st Parachute Regiment with the rank of Hauptmann.

Leonhard Schmidt joined the 2nd Company of the General Göring Regiment on November 3, 1937 and completed the parachutist-infantry course at Stendal. Following an NCO course in Stendal he joined 3rd Company, 1st Parachute Regiment before the outbreak of war. Schmidt served with the company in the campaign in Poland but saw no action. Promoted to *Oberjäger* on November 1, 1939, he saw action in the Stavanger area in April 1940 and received the Iron Cross, Second Class. In the campaign in Western Europe he fought with 3rd Company and won the Iron Cross, First Class.

Schmidt was wounded during the airborne invasion of Crete on May 20, 1941. Following his convalescence he rejoined his company; the 1st Parachute Regiment was now stationed in the northern sector of the Eastern Front. Schmidt was wounded again near Schlüsselburg on November 15; on January 1, 1942 he was promoted to *Feldwebel.*

The regiment's second tour in Russia saw him in the combat zone southwest of Orel. *Feldwebel* Schmidt was one of the aces of the regiment. He seized the well-defended village of Promklevo. Further actions followed, the most significant being a counterattack in the area of Baldysh and Dimitrovsk on March 4, 1942. Schmidt put the run to the enemy and took over 100 prisoners. Further successes included the capture of Aleshenka and the battle for the enemy-held Hills 266 and 262.3. On April 20, 1943 Schmidt was promoted to *Leutnant* for bravery in the face of the enemy.

Schmidt fought successfully in the Italian theater, at Ortona as well as at Cassino. Once again he received an early promotion, to the rank of *Oberleutnant.* Leonhard Schmidt won the Knight's Cross on April 30, 1945 during the fighting withdrawal by the German forces.

WERNER HERBERT SCHMIDT

Born on October 1, 1906 in Posen.
Ultimate rank: Oberstleutnant.
Last service position: Commander of the 3rd Parachute Replacement and Training Regiment.
German Cross in Gold on May 4, 1942.
Knight's Cross on April 5, 1944 as commander of the 1st Parachute Machine-gun Battalion, 1st Parachute Division with the rank of Major.

Werner Herbert Schmidt entered Brandenburg-Havel Police School on April 5, 1927. After various courses and postings he became a Police *Oberwachtmeister* on October 18, 1930.

On April 20, 1934 followed his promotion to Police *Leutnant*. Two days earlier he had been transferred to the Wecke Special-Purpose Police Battalion.

Schmidt requested a transfer to the Luftwaffe, which took place on October 1, 1935. On March 1, 1938 he became a *Hauptmann* and commander of 12th Company, 1st Parachute Regiment, with which he saw action in the invasion of Holland. Named company commander of the 1st Parachute Machine-gun Battalion's 3rd Company on September 1, 1940, he and his company saw action in the airborne invasion of Crete. Schmidt won both Iron Crosses in the operation. Promoted to *Major* on October 1, 1941, on February 6, 1942 he became commanding officer of the 1st Parachute Machine-gun Battalion. Schmidt led the battalion in action in the central sector of the Eastern Front, where he received the German Cross in Gold following a number of major successes.

Following the allied invasion of Sicily, on July 13 Schmidt and his battalion were flown to Catania airfield in He 111 transport aircraft. The battalion took up position near Primasole, where it opposed a landing by the British 1st Parachute Brigade and inflicted heavy losses on the enemy.

At Cassino *Major* Schmidt and his men defended the slopes around the monastery and repulsed an assault by the 4th Indian Division. Schmidt was badly wounded in the fighting and was awarded the Knight's Cross.

On the trip to the Mallersdorf Reserve Hospital Schmidt knew that for him the war was over. On December 1, 1944 he was promoted to *Oberstleutnant*.

WOLF WERNER GRAF VON DER SCHULENBURG

Born on September 14, 1899 in Berlin-Charlottenburg.
Ultimate rank: Oberstleutnant.
Last service position: Commanding officer of the 13th Parachute Regiment.
Knight's Cross on June 20, 1943 as commander of I Battalion, 1st Parachute Regiment with the rank of Major.
Killed on July 14, 1944 near St. James, Normandy.

Wolf Werner von der Schulenburg joined the Imperial Army as a war volunteer in 1917. He was badly wounded during the fighting on the Western Front. Von der Schulenburg was promoted to *Leutnant* on September 1, 1918.

Called up on August 15, 1939, at his own request he joined the 1st Parachute Regiment as an ordnance officer and took part in the campaign against Poland.

Von der Schulenburg participated in the fighting in Fortress Holland. He won both Iron Crosses in the course of his regiment's operations in the Moerdijk-Dordrecht area and received promotion to *Hauptmann* on November 1, 1940.

In Crete von der Schulenburg served with III Battalion, 1st Parachute Regiment, providing exemplary support to the battalion commander, *Major* Karl-Lothar Schulz.

During the campaign against Russia von der Schulenburg received his promotion to *Major* on December 19, 1941 while serving in the northern sector at the Neva River. He received his first command on February 20, 1942, when he was placed in command of the 1st Parachute Regiment's I Battalion. He led the battalion until April 21, 1944.

Von der Schulenburg was at the height of his skill during the second tour in Russia. Following numerous successful actions, on June 20, 1943 he was awarded the Knight's Cross. Near Orel and Dimitrovsk his battalion fought under the command of the 78th Assault Division, whose commander recommended him for the Knight's Cross.

In Italy, especially in the Monte Cassino combat zone, von der Schulenburg again fought in a defensive role under his old friend Karl-Lothar Schmidt. On April 21, 1944, before the invasion in the Seine Bay, he became commander of the 13th Parachute Regiment. He was killed in action on July 14, 1944 while fighting at the head of his regiment. Von der Schulenburg was posthumously promoted to *Oberleutnant* on July 23, 1944.

KARL-LOTHAR SCHULZ

Born on April 30, 1907.
Ultimate rank: Generalmajor.
Last service position: Commander of the 1st Parachute Division.
German Cross in Gold on March 9, 1942.
Knight's Cross on May 24, 1940 as commander of III Battalion, 1st Parachute Regiment with the rank of Hauptmann.
Oak Leaves (459th recipient) on April 20, 1944 as commander of the 1st Parachute Regiment with the rank of Oberst.
Swords (112th recipient) on November 18, 1944 as commander of the 1st Parachute Division with the rank of Oberst.
Died on September 26, 1972 in Wiesbaden.

After completing school Karl-Lothar Schulz reported to the 1st Artillery Regiment in Königsberg, where he was trained as a pioneer. In January 1925 he entered the police service and on February 25, 1933 transferred to the Wecke Special Purpose Police Battalion, where he served as a platoon commander. Schulz became a *Leutnant* on March 20, 1934 and following the incorporation of the police group into the General Göring State Police Regiment joined the 15 (Pioneer) Company as company commander.

After taking a parachutist-rifleman course Schulz took his company, which had volunteered for the move, into IV (Parachutist-Infantry) Battalion, General Göring Regiment.

On January 1, 1940 *Hauptmann* Schulz was placed in command of III Battalion, 1st Parachute Regiment. In the western campaign Schulz's battalion captured Rotterdam airport, which was vitally important for the landing of follow-up troops. Schulz was awarded the Knight's Cross.

Promoted to *Major* on July 19, 1940, Schulz was dropped near Heraklion. He led his forces into the city, however a shortage of ammunition forced him to abandon it soon afterward. Schulz nevertheless held positions near Heraklion.

On September 29, 1941 Schulz led III Battalion, 1st Parachute Regiment into the Leningrad battle zone. The unit fought at the Neva River at great cost. Schulz subsequently assumed command of the 1st Parachute Regiment, which he led in the regiment's second tour of duty in Russia.

Following the allied landing on the Italian mainland Schulz saw action at Tarent. He distinguished himself as a commander at Anzio-Nettuno and Cassino and during the fighting withdrawal to Bologna and won the Oak Leaves and the Swords. On January 17, 1945 Schulz was promoted to *Generalmajor*.

ERICH SCHUSTER

**Born on November 6, 1919 in Norbach, Bernkastel District, Mosel.
Ultimate rank: Oberleutnant (promoted posthumously).
Last service position: Commander of 1st Company, 5th Parachute
Regiment in Tunisia.
Knight's Cross on August 21, 1941 as a squad leader in 3rd Company,
1st Parachute Assault Regiment with the rank of Feldwebel.
Killed in action on November 11, 1943 on Hill 311 in Tunisia.**

Erich Schuster joined the parachute troops as a volunteer on October 3,
1938. He completed the parachutist-rifleman course at Stendal Parachute
School and on December 3, 1938 was transferred to 1st Company, 1st Parachute Regiment.

On November 12, 1939 Schuster was transferred to the Koch Parachute Assault Battalion. His first combat parachute action was with Assault
Group Stahl on May 10, 1940. The group's objective was Veldwezelt Bridge.
Schuster distinguished himself as a squad leader and on May 13 received
both Iron Crosses.

On May 20, 1941 *Oberjäger* Schuster and his squad landed with the
glider group at Malemes airfield. When his platoon leader, *Feldwebel* Arpke,
was put out of action when his glider crashed on landing, Schuster assumed command. He eliminated a flak battery and occupied the western
end of Malemes airfield. For these actions he was decorated with the Knight's
Cross.

Schuster was promoted to Feldwebel on July 25, 1941 and in January
1942 went to Russia as a platoon commander. His 3rd Company was now
led by *Oberleutnant* Hoefeld, who had replaced *Oberleutnant* von Plessen,
who was killed on Crete. The company took part in the defense of Anisovo-
Gorodische airfield. When *Leutnant* Arpke took part in a counterattack toward Mithinka by 3rd Company his friend Schuster was also there. Arpke
was killed and Schuster assumed command.

With the formation of the 5th Parachute Regiment Schuster, now a
Leutnant, took command of the 1st Company, which he led in action in
Tunisia. He was killed in action on January 11, 1943 during an advance
over Hill 311. On April 8, 1943 Schuster was posthumously promoted to
Oberleutnant for bravery in the face of the enemy.

ALFRED SCHWARZMANN

Born on March 23, 1912 in Fürth, Bavaria.
Ultimate rank: Major.
Last service position: Commander of the headquarters of the 1st Parachute Division.
Knight's Cross on May 29, 1940.

Alfred Schwarzmann joined the 13th Company of the Nuremberg Infantry Regiment on April 1, 1939 after signing up for a twelve-year period of service. He became an *Unteroffizier* on May 1, 1935 and was a member of the gymnastics team preparing for the Olympic Games in Berlin in 1936, where he won three gold medals.

Schwarzmann served as an army sports instructor at the Army Sport School in Wünsdorf. From there he went to II Battalion, 1st Parachute Regiment in Stendal on January 1, 1939 and later to Braunschweig. On March 11, 1940 he was promoted to *Oberleutnant* and on April 1 became commander of a machine-gun platoon in the 8th Company of the 1st Parachute Regiment.

On May 10, 1940 Schwarzmann and his company parachuted into Holland and took a key enemy position on the coast. This they held until relief forces arrived. In the course of the fighting Schwarzmann was badly wounded when a bullet pierced a lung.

Alfred Schwarzmann received both Iron Crosses on May 25, 1940 and four days later the Knight's Cross.

On Crete Schwarzmann saw action in the Heraklion area. Promoted to *Hauptmann* on June 27, 1942, he led the 3rd Parachute Regiment's 8th Company and was later made company commander. Schwarzmann fought in Russia in 1941-42.

On March 15, 1943 he became commander of the headquarters of the 7th Air Division. Afterward he received the same position with the 1st Parachute Division.

Schwarzmann was forced to enter the Luftwaffe hospital in Munich on March 4, 1944 because of his old wound. On April 20, 1945 he was promoted to *Major.* Schwarzmann was held by the British from May 9 to October 29, 1945.

Schwarzmann took part in the 1952 Olympic Games in Helsinki as a forty-year-old and won a silver medal.

GÜNTHER SEMPERT

Born on October 20, 1918 in Wechselburg an der Mulde, Saxony.
Ultimate rank: Major.
Last service position: Commander of the 1st Parachute Anti-tank Battalion.
German Cross in Gold on June 14, 1944.
Knight's Cross on September 30, 1944 as commander of the 1st Parachute Anti-tank Battalion with the rank of Hauptmann.

Sempert joined the 4th Anti-tank Battalion's 3rd Company as an officer candidate on November 2, 1937. He completed the 22nd Replacement Officer Course in Munich and on August 2, 1939 joined 3rd Company, 4th Anti-tank Battalion, where he became a *Leutnant* on December 22, 1939. Sempert served in Poland while still an officer candidate and was wounded near Ilza.

Soon after his promotion to *Leutnant* Sempert joined the parachute troops and completed the parachutist-rifleman course in Braunschweig.

Sempert parachuted into Crete as leader of the 1st Platoon of 1st Company, 7th Parachute Anti-tank Battalion and was wounded in the subsequent fighting. He received both Iron Crosses. On December 1, 1941 he became an *Oberleutnant* and served as commander of 5th Company, 7th Parachute Anti-tank Battalion in the central sector of the Eastern Front from October 20, 1942 until March 31, 1943. He and his company destroyed 67 enemy bunkers.

Earlier Sempert had lost an eye to exploding ammunition while surveying the battlefield at Dieppe. However this did not prevent him from seeing further action.

Sempert played a decisive part in the freeing of Mussolini from the Gran Sasso. For this and his company's efforts in the defensive struggle in souther Italy he was awarded the German Cross in Gold. Sempert was promoted to *Hauptmann* on May 5, 1944 during the Third Battle of Cassino. All told he and his battalion destroyed more than 120 enemy tanks, as a result of which Sempert was decorated with the Knight's Cross.

On May 2, 1945 Sempert was captured by the Americans and made a prisoner of war.

HUBERT SNIERS

Born on April 6, 1915 in Rheydt, Rhineland.
Ultimate rank: Oberleutnant.
Last service position: Commander of III Battalion, 15th Parachute Regiment.
Knight's Cross on October 24, 1944 as signals officer as well as commander of 9th Company, 15th Parachute Regiment with the rank of Leutnant.

Sniers joined the Kriegsmarine on October 1, 1936 after completing his period of labor service. He was trained as a radio operator and was assigned to the *Admiral Scheer* as a *Gefreiter*. One year later he was transferred to the flying boat base at Parow as an *Obergefreiter* and radio operator. He became a radio technician and *Funkmeister* (technical sergeant) and on May 20, 1941 was named a wartime officer candidate. Sniers reported to the parachute troops on July 3, 1941; after completing the course for parachutist-riflemen he was assigned to the 4th Parachute Regiment.

In March 1942 he was sent to the Luftwaffe officer candidate school in Gross-Born, where he received his *Leutnant's* shoulder boards on April 20, 1942.

Sniers saw action in Russia in the summer of 1943 as signals and operations officer with III Battalion, 4th Parachute Regiment. He won the Iron Cross, Second Class there on September 7, 1943. On January 1, 1944 he was transferred to the 15th Parachute Regiment. On January 29, 1944 he received the Iron Cross, First Class for his actions in Italy.

From June 21, 1944 Sniers led 9th Company of the 15th Parachute Regiment on the invasion front. The 5th Parachute Division, to which this regiment belonged, was transferred into the Cotentin area on July 10. West of Carentan the 15th Regiment, now under the command of the 353rd Infantry Division, fought with determination and withdrew only slowly before the superior US forces.

In the course of the fighting Sniers, by now an *Oberleutnant*, was wounded. Nevertheless he assumed command of the battalion at the beginning of August following the wounding of its commanding officer and achieved great success in a defensive role, which won him the Knight's Cross. Sniers and his battalion withdrew fighting into the Reich, where he was taken prisoner.

ALBERT STECKEN

Born on January 24, 1915 in Münster, Westphalia.
Ultimate rank: General Staff Major.
Last service position: Ia of the 8th Parachute Division.
Spanish Cross in Gold with Swords on June 6, 1939.
Knight's Cross on April 28, 1945 as Ia of the 8th Parachute Division
with the rank of General Staff Major.

Stecken joined the Duisburg-Hambörn State Police on October 5, 1934 and on July 1, 1935 arrived at the Luftwaffe Officer Candidate School in Potsdam-Eiche. On May 1, 1936 he was transferred to the Flak-Artillery School in Wüstrow as an *Oberfähnrich.*

From I Battalion, 8th Flak Regiment Stecken joined the Condor Legion's motorized flak battalion on March 15, 1938. By now a *Leutnant,* he took part in the fighting during the second Ebro offensive and the first and second Mediterranean offensives. Stecken received three Spanish decorations.

Stecken received the Iron Cross, First Class while serving with I Battalion, 32nd Flak Regiment in Berlin-Heiligensee. He was promoted to *Hauptmann* on November 1, 1941 and after a series of postings attended the first warfare course at the Academy of Air Warfare in Berlin-Gatow. After holding a number of staff positions he was taken into the Luftwaffe General Staff on June 23, 1943. On July 1 he was promoted to *Major.*

From November 16, 1943 until October 6, 1944 Stecken was the Ia of the 23rd Flak Division and subsequently Ia of the 606th Special Purpose Division. In this capacity he saw action in the central sector of the Eastern Front.

Assigned to the staff of the Head of the Luftwaffe's Technical Equipment Branch on January 11, 1945, on January 15 he took over the position of Ia of the 8th Parachute Division. With it he fought on the Lower Rhine front. Stecken led a hastily-assembled group of forces in a counterattack against enemy forces which had broken through near Empel-Millingen and restored the main line of resistance. Stecken was decorated with the Knight's Cross for this decisive feat of arms following a recommendation by *General* Meindl.

EDGAR STENTZLER

Born on March 27, 1905 in Dortmund.
Ultimate rank: Major.
Last service position: Commander of III Battalion, Parachute Assault Regiment.
Knight's Cross on July 9, 1941 as commander of III Battalion, Parachute Assault Regiment with the rank of Major.
Died in hospital in Tilsit on October 19, 1941 after being badly wounded.

Stentzler joined the 1st Cavalry Regiment's 1st Squadron on April 1, 1923. There he was promoted to *Leutnant* on May 1, 1929. Stentzler transferred to the 15th Cavalry Regiment and on October 1, 1931 joined the 2nd Company of the regiment's Anti-tank Squadron.

Stentzler was one of the Wehrmacht's outstanding riders, winning numerous competitions. In 1936 alone he won nine jump competitions and several dressage meets.

On October 31, 1933 Stentzler left the army as an *Oberleutnant* and moved to the Luftwaffe. His next stations were Celle Flying School, Grossenhain Flying Staffel and the 121st Reconnaissance Gruppe in Neuhaus. On August 1, 1935 he was promoted to *Hauptmann*.

After successfully attending the Academy of Air warfare, on June 20, 1940 Stentzler joined the Parachute Replacement Battalion as a volunteer. He completed parachute training and on July 13, 1940 became commanding officer of II Battalion, Parachute Assault Battalion in Quedlinburg, where he was promoted to *Major* six days later.

Stentzler and his battalion jumped over Crete east of Malemes. He took part in the capture of Hill 107 and on the evening of May 20 assumed command of the regiment in place of the badly-wounded *Generalmajor* Meindl until *Oberst* Ramcke arrived.

Stentzler received the Knight's Cross for his actions on Crete. During the fighting on the Neva front in the winter of 1941 he was badly wounded in an assault from the Petrushino bridgehead on October 3 and subsequently died in hospital in Tilsit on October 19.

KURT STEPHANI

Born on August 15, 1904 in Donaueschingen, Baden.
Ultimate rank: Major.
Last service position: Commanding officer of the 9th Parachute Regiment.
German Cross in Gold on June 5, 1944.
Knight's Cross on September 30, 1944 as commanding officer of the 9th Parachute Regiment with the rank of Major.
Killed in action near Trun-Chambrois, France on August 20, 1944.

Stephani joined the Reichswehr on October 1, 1923 and served in the Ulm Artillery Regiment. On April 23, 1935, after completing his period of labor service, he took part in his first exercise as a reservist, an officer preparation course, at Döberitz Infantry School.

Commanding the school at that time was *Oberstleutnant* Hans Hube. Further reserve exercises followed and on November 1, 1937 Stephani was promoted to *Leutnant*.

After serving in the home war zone, Belgium and France, Stephani saw action in Russia from June 22, 1941 to August 28, 1942. On October 10, 1941 he became commander of the 9th (Machine-gun) Company, 75th Light Infantry Regiment and won the Iron Cross, First Class on June 28, 1942. Stephani was promoted to *Hauptmann* on June 16, 1942.

On September 1, 1942 Stephani was appointed commander of the reconnaissance units of XIII Fliegerkorps. Soon afterward he became commander of the 12th Parachute Reconnaissance Battalion and on January 1, 1943 transferred to the Luftwaffe. On February 1, 1944 he took over the 9th Parachute Regiment of the 3rd Parachute Division as commanding officer.

Stephani and his unit saw action in Normandy. On July 11, near Bois de Cerisy – Hill 192 – St. André – Caumont, he held the right wing of the division against an enemy attack carried out by strong armored forces. The division was able to break out of the Falaise Pocket between Trun and Chambois thanks to the efforts of the 9th Regiment. Stephani, who was badly wounded during the fighting, was awarded the Knight's Cross for his regiment's accomplishment. He subsequently died of his wounds on August 20.

GÜNTHER STRAEHLER-POHL

Born on July 29, 1917 in Breslau, Silesia.
Ultimate rank: Hauptmann.
Last service position: Commander of Battle Group Straehler-Pohl.
Knight's Cross on May 10, 1943 as commander of Battle Group Straehler-Pohl with the rank of Hauptmann.
Died on July 31, 1980 in Wildeshausen, Lower Saxony.

Straehler-Pohl entered the Luftwaffe Officer candidate School in Frankenstein on March 28, 1935. After serving with the 28th Infantry Regiment in Oppeln he went to Dresden Officer Candidate School. Straehler-Pohl became an *Oberfähnrich* on October 1, 1936 and on April 1, 1937 was promoted to *Leutnant*.

After several more courses Streahler-Pohl reported to the parachute troops and completed the army's parachutist-rifleman course in Stendal before joining the Stendal Parachute Infantry Battalion on August 1, 1938.

On January 1, 1939 Straehler-Pohl was taken into II Battalion, 1st Parachute Regiment. He saw his first combat at Wola-Gulowska in Poland.

Straehler-Pohl went into the Western Campaign as commander of 5th Company, 1st Parachute Regiment. He and his company came down near the Moerdijk bridges inside Fortress Holland. On May 23, 1940 he received both Iron Crosses.

Straehler-Pohl took part in the invasion of Crete with his company. From October 1941 they fought in Russia, in the Neva River combat zone.

Promoted to *Hauptmann* on March 26, 1942, Straehler-Pohl saw action in North Africa with the Ramcke Parachute Brigade, taking part in its successful passage through enemy-held territory to Fuka following the Battle of El Alamein.

Following the successful landings in West Africa by the western allies Straehler-Pohl fought on the Tunisian front. He and his battle group fought a bitter battle against American forces at Hamman Lif. Straehler-Pohl's actions there won him the Knight's Cross on May 10, 1943. He was unable to receive the award as he had been captured on May 8 in the battle for the Tunis bridgehead. Straehler-Pohl was released in Germany at the end of 1947.

GENERALOBERST KURT STUDENT

Kurt Student served under three entirely different forms of government in his military life: the Empire, the Weimar Republic and the "Third Reich." But in his heart he was and remained a monarchist. Hitler and Göring knew this and respected it.

Student was born in Neumark on May 12, 1890, the son of the owner of a manorial estate. In 1901 he and his four brothers became Prussian cadets. Student received his commission as a *Leutnant* on June 24, 1909, and in 1913 he reported to Berlin-Johannisthal for pilot training. By autumn he was one of the "old eagles."

As a reconnaissance and bomber pilot, and finally as a fighter pilot and leader of Jagdstaffel 9, Student received the Knight's Cross of the House Order of Hohenzollern. On June 20, 1918 be was promoted to *Hauptmann.*

On April 1, 1920 Student joined the Reichswehr's newly formed aviation group, Truppenflieger-Staffel 120, where he served as technical advisor.

In 1922 Student emerged the victor in the Round Saxony Flight, flying an Albatros L 69.

After a three-year tour of duty with the field forces Student returned to the Reichswehrministerium. He became commander of technical schools, commander of the Rechlin Test Center, inspector of flying schools in Berlin and finally senior Air Commander 3 in Münster, Westphalia.

On April 1, 1938 Student was promoted to *Generalmajor* and made commander of the 3rd Air Division. He had already established contact with the Stendal Parachute School by this time. This was followed on July 1, 1938 by Student's surprise appointment as the commander of German Parachute Troops. Student was now in charge of the youngest branch of the German Armed Forces. He also oversaw its creation, for on September 1, 1938 the first parachute division was formed, which for reasons of secrecy received the title "7th Air Division."

Student directed special attention at equipping the 7th Air Division with heavy weapons: air-landed artillery, flak and anti-tank guns.

When the Second World War broke out the German parachute and airborne troops were in the midst of their development.

The key to the success and the homogeneity of these forces lay in their training as soldiers and the fact that they were all volunteers.

The parachute troops saw no action in the Polish Campaign. On October 27, 1939 Hitler briefed Student on the missions he had in mind for them. The parachute and airborne troops were to go into action in the Western Campaign. Their missions were:

1. Take the Belgian fortress of Eben Emael on the Albert Canal.
2. Seize the bridges across the Albert Canal and hold them until the arrival of army units.

Together with *Oberst* Bruno Bräuer, commander of the 1st Parachute Regiment, Student selected *Hauptmann* Walter Koch for the action at the Albert Canal and *Oberleutnant* Witzig for the assault on Eben Emael.

Promoted to *Generalleutnant* on January 1, 1940, Student led both of these actions, which took the enemy completely by surprise, to success.

Generalleutnant Student was badly wounded in Rotterdam and was put completely out of action for eight months. On January 25, 1941 a healthy Student reported to Hitler in Berchtesgaden.

On September 2 Student visited Karinhall for the first time since being wounded. There he received the Golden Pilots Badge with Diamonds from *Reichsmarschall* Göring. It was a decoration which was given to only about 40 persons.

Göring instructed Student to evaluate further air landing possibilities. In the period that followed he took over the formation and command of the Air Landing Corps formed from the 7th Air Division and the army's 22nd Airborne Division. For reasons of secrecy the corps was designated XI Fliegerkorps.

On April 20, 1941 *Generalleutnant* Student flew to see Hitler in his forward headquarters at Semmering. He proposed to Hitler that they take the island of Crete from the air, because this was the first springboard to the Suez Canal.

Hitler agreed to the Crete operation, which began on May 20, 1941. In place of the 22nd Airborne Division, which was in action elsewhere, the 5th Mountain Infantry Division under *Generalmajor* Julius Ringel was selected for the airborne landing operation. Crete was captured by May 30, but the parachute troops suffered very heavy losses. These losses caused Hitler to dispense with further paratroop actions.

Although Hitler considered *General* Student's proposals for Operation "Hercules" (the conquest of Malta) basically sound, they were rejected. At the conclusion of their discussions Hitler said, "This attack on Malta will not be carried out in 1942."

The 2nd Parachute Division was formed at the end of January 1943. In November of the previous year all the cover designations had been dropped and the 7th Air Division was now called the 1st Parachute Division.

In autumn 1942 the Ramcke Parachute Brigade went to Africa, becoming the first parachute unit to see action there. It was followed in November 1942 by the 5th Parachute Regiment under *Oberstleutnant* Koch, which was deployed in Tunisia. Other parachute units had been committed in an infantry role in Russia since autumn 1941.

At the end of June 1943 XI Fliegerkorps was stationed in France as a strategic reserve. The first contingents were sent to Sicily following the allied invasion of the island, however Sicily was lost.

On September 12, 1943 *General* Student led the operation to free the Duce from the Campo Imperatore mountain hotel on the Gran Sasso.

Italy withdrew from the Axis alliance on September 8. The paratroops of the 2nd Parachute Division freed themselves from encirclement by the Italians and occupied Rome. On September 11 all Italian forces in the area of Rome laid down their weapons.

The fighting in southern Italy, the Battle of Monte Cassino and the attempted defense against the allied landings at Anzio-Nettuno saw the paratroops in action in a defensive role.

On August 11, 1944 Kurt Student was promoted to *Generaloberst*. He had assumed command of the newly-formed First Parachute Army, which was under the command of Army Group B.

Generaloberst Student was in his command post south of Vught near Hertogenbosch when the allies launched Operation "Market Garden" on September 17. He personally led the defensive measures against the American 101st Airborne Division. The allied operation failed to reach its declared objectives.

Under *Generaloberst* Student the 1st Parachute Army fought in the Reichswald and in the defense of the Rhine, suffering heavy losses. At the end of April 1945 Student was named Commander-in-Chief of Army Group Vistula. The army group was cut off. Driving straight through three enemy divisions, *Generaloberst* Student reached Flensburg on the morning of May 9 and reported to *Grossadmiral* Dönitz.

After a number of years in prison Student returned to Germany. When the Association of German Parachute Troops was formed in 1949, Kurt Student became its president, a position he held until his death on July 1, 1978.

In 1962 his former opponents in Crete, the New Zealand Veterans Association, named him their vice-president.

Decorations:
Knight of the House Order of Hohenzollern: summer 1917
Knight's Cross of the Iron Cross on May 12, 1940
Golden Pilots Badge with Diamonds on September 2, 1941
Knight's Cross with Oak Leaves (305th recipient) on Sept. 27, 1943

ALFRED STURM

Born on August 23, 1888 in Saarbrücken.
Ultimate rank: Generalleutnant.
Last service position: Head of the Wehrmacht Motor Transport Service.
Iron Cross, First Class on January 17, 1917 (First World War).
Knight's Cross on July 9, 1941.
Died on March 8, 1962 in Detmold, Westphalia.

Alfred Sturm entered Bieberich NCO School on October 17, 1905. He entered the First World War as a *Vizefeldwebel* and from the 144th Infantry Regiment went to the Luftwaffe as an acting officer. He scored his first aerial victories with Jagdstaffel 5. Sturm was awarded the Iron Cross, First Class on January 17, 1917. On June 13, 1917 he was shot down in a duel with a British opponent.

After the war Sturm remained with the Reichswehr and was promoted to *Leutnant* on June 5, 1919. He became an *Oberleutnant* on January 15, 1921, an *Hauptmann* on March 1, 1926 and on January 1, 1926 became company commander of 6th Company, 8th Prussian Infantry Regiment.

Following his release from the army he joined the Luftwaffe and served as a an air observer. He soon returned to army service before joining the Luftwaffe again on October 1, 1933. Sturm served at the fighter school in Schleissheim and held command positions in Magdeburg and Detmold. He was promoted to *Major* on April 21, 1935 and *Oberstleutnant* on August 2, 1936.

On June 30, 1940 Sturm went to the Wittstock Parachute School. Although 52 years old he underwent the tough training and a month later was already leading the 2nd Parachute Regiment.

Sturm jumped with his regiment at the Corinth Canal and prevented ten-thousand British and Greek troops from escaping to Crete. On the second day of the invasion of Crete Sturm was captured by the British. His regiment fought with success under the command of *Major* Kroh. Sturm received the Knight's Cross.

Sturm was promoted to *Generalleutnant* on August 1, 1943. After holding a series of posts he was named Head of the Wehrmacht Motor Transport Service. Although released from the Wehrmacht on January 21, 1945 Sturm was arrested on April 23, 1945 and held illegally as a prisoner of war.

KARL STEPHAN TANNERT

Born on December 22, 1910 in Psaar, Loben District, Upper Silesia.
Ultimate rank: Oberstleutnant.
Last service position: Second in command, 2nd Parachute Regiment in Brest.
German Cross in Gold on March 11, 1942.
Knight's Cross on April 5, 1944.
Twice recommended for the Oak Leaves.

Tannert joined the Reichswehr on August 1, 1932, initially serving in the Upper Silesian Frontier Guard under *Major* von Rothkirch. On October 1, 1933 he became a term volunteer in 15th Company, 8th Infantry Regiment, Liegnitz. Tannert was transferred to the 74th Infantry Regiment on August 27, 1938 and there advanced to *Oberleutnant* on September 19, 1938.

On June 21, 1939 Tannert joined the parachute troops as a volunteer, completed the 18th Parachutist-Infantry Course in Stendal and was subsequently assigned to I Battalion, 1st Parachute Regiment.

The battalion fought in Denmark, where Tannert took part in the capture of the bridges near Masnedö. He parachuted into Holland as commander of the leading platoon of 1st Company, 1st Parachute Regiment. Tannert distinguished himself there and received the Iron Cross, First Class for his actions at Dordrecht. He also fought in Norway as part of the effort to relieve the 3rd Mountain Infantry Division in Narvik. On September 1, 1940 Tannert was named company commander of 1st Company, 1st Parachute Regiment.

Tannert led his company when it parachuted into Crete, where he was badly wounded on May 21, 1941. He nevertheless returned to action in northern Russia in the winter of 1941. At Gorodok in the Vyborgskaya bridgehead he sealed off and destroyed a group of enemy forces which had broken into the German positions. For this he received the German Cross in Gold.

Following his promotion to *Hauptmann*, Tannert and III Battalion, 2nd Parachute Regiment fought in the southern sector of the Eastern Front, where he won the Knight's Cross.

In Fortress Brest Tannert was second in command of the 2nd Parachute Regiment and held the enemy until September 19, 1944. Taken prisoner, he was not released until June 28, 1948.

HANS TEUSEN

Born on July 26, 1917 in Salz, Westerwald District.
Ultimate rank: Major.
Last service position: 1st Operations Officer in Army Group Student.
German Cross in Gold on September 10, 1944.
Knight's Cross on June 14, 1941 as a platoon leader in 6th Company, 2nd Parachute Regiment with the rank of Leutnant.

Hans Teusen joined the 4th Flak Regiment, Dortmund as an officer candidate on July 1, 1937. After attending the Luftwaffe Officer Candidate School in Werder and a subsequent parachutist-rifleman course in Wittstock-Dosse, on November 29, 1939 he joined the 2nd Parachute Regiment. There he took over 2nd Company and on December 28 was promoted to *Leutnant.*

Teusen led a platoon in the airborne assault on Corinth Canal. Delivered to the canal in gliders, the platoon eliminated a flak battery at the southern end of the crossing over Corinth Canal but was unable to prevent the bridge from being blown up.

Teusen and his platoon stormed into Corinth. There his company commander, *Hauptmann* Schirmer, ordered him to set out in the direction of Nauplia as the advance detachment. Teusen was wounded during the attack toward the south. 72 officers and 1,200 men surrendered to his platoon. Teusen was awarded the Knight's Cross.

On October 1, 1941 Teusen became adjutant of II Battalion, 2nd Parachute Regiment and on March 1, 1943 took over the regiment's 9th Company as company commander. Promoted to *Hauptmann* on September 1, 1943, Teusen saw action at the Mius River. The train taking 2nd Parachute Regiment back to Germany was halted in Gumbinnen and the unit was thrown into the hellish battle at the Volkhov.

Following a brief period in Italy the regiment returned to Russia in November 1943. Teusen was severely wounded near Zhitomir.

On May 1, 1944 Teusen took command of I Battalion, 16th Parachute Regiment/East, which he led in heavy fighting. As battalion commander he won the German Cross in Gold. When the war ended Teusen was Operations Officer of the First Parachute Army.

CORD TIETJEN

**Born on November 10, 1914 in Danzig-Langfuhr, Danzig District.
Ultimate rank: Hauptmann.
Last service position: Commander of 2nd Company, Corps Parachute
Pioneer Battalion and the Ia of the Ramcke Parachute Brigade.
Knight's Cross on May 24, 1940 as a platoon leader in 5th Company,
1st Parachute Regiment with the rank of Leutnant.**

Tietjen joined the 2nd Company of the 20th Pioneer Battalion in Hamburg-Harburg on October 20, 1936. On October 9, 1937 he was transferred to the Parachute Infantry Company, Stendal. He ended his parachute training with the army on December 17, 1937.

Effective December 31, 1938 Tietjen was taken on strength by the parachute troops. He had earlier been promoted to *Feldwebel* on October 1, 1938.

On January 28, 1939 Tietjen joined 5th Company, 1st Parachute Regiment in Braunschweig as a platoon leader. With this unit he took part in the campaign in Poland.

Tietjen was promoted to *Leutnant* on May 7, 1940. On May 10 he parachuted into Fortress Holland with II Battalion, 1st Parachute Regiment and landed near the Maas bridge near Doerdrecht. His company commander, *Oberleutnant* Straehler-Pohl, led the "Fifth" as it stormed the north end of the road bridge and occupied the bunkers located there. Tietjen led the way in the dash across the bridge. He and his platoon had landed at the south end of the span. They overpowered the bridge guards and took possession of the earth bunkers and nearby dikes. Tietjen was wounded in the process. For his actions he was awarded both Iron Crosses.

Two days later, when his feats at the bridge became known, Tietjen was awarded the Knight's Cross.

On September 29, 1940 Tietjen took over the 1st Company of the 7th Parachute Pioneer Battalion as company commander. By now an *Oberleutnant*, he led the company in the battle for Crete. In the Ramcke Brigade he assumed command of the 2nd Company of the Corps Parachute Pioneer Battalion. Tietjen was captured while serving with the brigade and was finally released on February 11, 1947 following an odyssey through Egypt, Canada and England.

ERICH TIMM

Born on February 15, 1913 in Königsberg, Prussia.
Ultimate rank: Oberstleutnant.
Last service position: Commander of the 12th Parachute Assault Regiment.
Knight's Cross on October 3, 1944 as leader of the 12th Parachute Assault Regiment (4th Parachute Division) with the rank of Major.

Erich Timm joined the state police on April 1, 1933 and served initially at the police school in Brandenburg-Havel. Promoted to *Leutnant* on April 1, 1935, on July 7 he was transferred to the Luftwaffe and served with the 12th Flak Regiment's 4th Company in Lankwitz near Berlin.

After a series of postings, on June 1, 1940 Timm voluntarily reported to 1st Company, Anti-aircraft Machine-gun Battalion in Halberstadt as company commander. He took the parachute course at Wittstock-Dosse Parachute School and on April 26, 1941 became company commander of 1st Company, Parachute Anti-aircraft Machine-gun Battalion.

Timm had won both Iron Crosses in Holland as commander of the 106th Light Flak Battery. He was seriously wounded in the fighting on Crete on May 20 and on June 1, 1941 he was promoted to the rank of *Hauptmann.*

Timm returned to the front-line troops in February 1943. On August 1 he was named commander of I Battalion, Parachute Assault Regiment. Promoted to *Major* on October 1, 1943, he served as regimental commander during the dramatic events in southern Russia in the winter of 1943-44.

Timm led the parachute Assault Regiment's II Battalion at Anzio-Nettuno. He and his regiment distinguished themselves at the Futa Pass as well as at the Senio and in the area east of Velletri. Timm was named in the Wehrmacht communique after repulsing a large-scale attack by the American 34th Infantry Division on both sides of Velletri. It was there that Timm won the Knight's Cross.

Promotion to *Oberstleutnant* followed on January 1, 1945 and Timm and his regiment fought a sacrificial battle as they withdrew through Italy. He was captured on April 28, 1945 and released on September 3 that same year.

RUDOLF TOSCHKA

Born on September 26, 1911 in Berlin-Wilmersdorf.
Ultimate rank: Hauptmann.
Last service position: Commander of I Battalion, Parachute Assault Regiment.
Knight's Cross on July 14, 1941 as leader of 1st Platoon, 1st Company, Airborne (Glider) Assault Regiment with the rank of Oberleutnant.
Killed on February 20, 1944 in the Anzio-Nettuno bridgehead.

Toschka entered Brandenburg-Havel Police School as a police candidate on October 6, 1931. On September 1, 1933 he became a member of 6th Company, General Göring State Police Group and was automatically taken into the General Göring Regiment on October 10, 1935. Toschka was promoted to *Feldwebel* on April 1, 1937 and *Oberfeldwebel* on February 1, 1940.

Toschka completed the parachutist-rifleman course on March 15, 1938, and on April 1 of that year he joined 1st Company, 1st Parachute Regiment as a platoon leader.

Toschka took part in the parachute and glider operations against the bridges over the Albert Canal and the fortress of Eben Emael. He was decorated with both Iron Crosses. On May 20, 1940 Toschka was promoted to *Leutnant* for bravery in the face of the enemy.

Oberleutnant Toschka took part in the Crete operation with his 1st Platoon, 1st Company of the 1st Parachute Regiment commanded by *Major* Koch. Ninety men in nine gliders near the flak positions at Suda and Chania and at Malemes airfield. Toschka and his platoon landed due south of Chania in the middle of an enemy formation. He destroyed the enemy troops there and put the flak battery out of action, but was badly wounded. Toschka was awarded the Knight's Cross for "opening the way to Chania."

Toschka was promoted to *Hauptmann* on October 14, 1942. After recovering from his wounds, on October 15, 1943 he took command of I Battalion, Parachute Assault Regiment and led the unit in action in Russia.

Toschka was killed in action on February 20, 1944 in the Anzio-Nettuno bridgehead.

HORST TREBES

Born on October 22, 1916 in Cologne.
Ultimate rank: Hauptmann.
Last service position: Commander of III Battalion, 6th Parachute Regiment.
Knight's Cross on July 9, 1941 as leader of III Battalion, 1st Parachute Assault Regiment with the rank of Oberleutnant.
Killed in action on July 29, 1944 in Normandy south of St. Denys-le-Gast.

Horst Trebes joined the Wehrmacht as an officer candidate on April 1, 1936 and by April 20, 1938 had attained the rank of *Leutnant*. On June 1, 1938 he joined the army's Parachute Infantry Battalion in Braunschweig and on April 1, 1939 was taken on strength by III Battalion, 1st Parachute Regiment in Gardelegen.

Trebes saw action in the Polish Campaign and received the Iron Cross, Second Class. During the campaign in Holland Trebes won the Iron Cross, First Class on May 23, 1940.

On Crete Trebes saw action as *Hauptmann* beim Stabe with III Battalion, 1st Parachute Assault Regiment. With *Major* Braun and his friend *Oberleutnant* Schächter, he formed a battle group from the regimental headquarters which landed at the large bridge due west of Malemes in nine gliders. The battle group was supposed to seize the bridge over the Tavronitis and set out to attack the flak position due west of the airfield with the support of I Battalion, 1st Parachute Regiment.

Trebes attacked at 11.00 hours on May 20 and freed *Leutnant* Kalhey's surrounded platoon. Trebes assumed command of the battle group after the death of *Major* Braun and the wounding of *Oberleutnant* Schächter. He and the rest of his battalion fought their way through to IV Battalion. Trebes attacked again on May 23 and stormed through as far as the stream bed west of Platanias, playing a part in the capture of Hill 107. This feat won him the Knight's Cross.

In Russia Trebes fought as company commander in III Battalion, 1st Parachute Assault Regiment. In early 1944 he took command of III Battalion of the 6th Parachute Regiment then being formed. He was killed in action in the bitter fighting near Carentan on September 27, 1944.

HEINRICH TRETTNER

Born on September 19, 1907 in Minden, Westphalia.
Ultimate rank: Generalleutnant.
Last service position: Commander of the 4th Parachute Division.
German Spanish Cross in Gold on June 6, 1939.
Knight's Cross on May 24, 1940 as Ia of the 7th Air Division with the rank of Major.
Oak Leaves (586th recipient) on September 17, 1944 as commander of the 4th Parachute Division with the rank of Generalmajor.
Deceased (date and location unknown).

Heinrich Trettner joined the Reichswehr's 18th Cavalry Regiment as an officer candidate on April 1, 1925. He passed through the Infantry School in Dresden and later the Cavalry School in Hannover. On September 30, 1932 he left the Reichswehr as an *Oberleutnant.* The next day he began his service at Braunschweig Flying School. Trettner joined the Reich Air Ministry on October 1, 1933 and subsequently served in various Luftwaffe agencies as an adjutant. On June 1, 1935 he was promoted to *Hauptmann.*

After completing the third course at the 2nd Air Warfare School in Berlin, Trettner joined the Condor Legion as IIa and adjutant to the legion's commander, *Oberst* von Richthofen. He went to Spain with the legion and on October 2, 1937 was named *Staffelkapitän* of 1./K 88.

Following general staff training, on July 1, 1938 Trettner was assigned to the Ia op of the 7th Air Division. On August 1, 1939 he became a *Major* and from June 15 served under *Generalmajor* Student as Ia of the 7th Air Division. He and Student worked out all the operations for the Western Campaign.

On September 2, 1942 Trettner became Chief-of-Staff of XI Fliegerkorps and on October 4, 1943 was given the job, at his request, of forming the 4th Parachute Division.

Trettner led his division at Anzio-Nettuno and was several times named in the Wehrmacht communique. On May 3, 1945, following the German surrender in Italy, he was taken prisoner by the British.

HERBERT TROTZ

Born on May 11, 1915 in Glatz, Lower Silesia.
Ultimate rank: Hauptmann.
Last service position: Commander of the Fortress Grenadier Regiment Trotz in Fortress Breslau.
Knight's Cross on April 30, 1945 as commander of the Fortress Grenadier Regiment *Trotz* with the rank of Hauptmann.
Died on July 31, 1980 in Bad Meinberg.

Herbert Trotz joined the 6th (Light Infantry) Company of the Prussian 7th Infantry Regiment in Glatz on April 1, 1933. After training as a radio operator he joined the East Prussian Air Transport Unit in Seerappen and later Neukuhren. On October 1, 1938 he became an *Oberfeldwebel* and took part in the fighting in Poland.

From June 22, 1941 until November 21, 1944 he saw action in the pitiless struggle on the Eastern Front with the Luftwaffe signals troops. On May 20, 1943 he was named company commander of the 2nd Company of the 203rd Luftwaffe Signals Regiment. A year later he became commander of 2nd Company, 57th Luftwaffe Signals Regiment. Twice wounded in Russia, on November 9, 1944 Trotz, now at the rank of *Hauptmann,* returned from Russia to Switchboard Detachment West of the 4th and then the 5th Jagddivision in Metz.

On November 22, 1944 Trotz went to parachute school in Goslar and Wittstock. He became company commander of 10th Company, 26th Parachute Regiment. Together with the rest of III Battalion, 26th Parachute Regiment, Trotz and his company were flown by Ju 52s into the surrounded fortress of Breslau from February 23 to 26, 1945. Trotz led his company in the unique defensive battle waged in the city. He fought up front with his men, whether in hand-to-hand combat in the sewers or in the ruins of buildings. On orders from *General* Niehoff he became leader of a battle group and in April 1945 stood in the center of the bitter struggle for the city. On April 30, 1945 he was awarded the Knight's Cross which he had long deserved.

On May 6, 1945, after the surrender of Breslau, Trotz was taken prisoner by the Soviets. He was released on August 7, 1949.

ALEXANDER UHLIG

Born on February 9, 1919 in Meusdorf Manor, Leipzig District.
Ultimate rank: Oberfeldwebel.
Last service position: Platoon leader in the 4th Company of the 6th Parachute Regiment.
Knight's Cross on October 29, 1944 as a platoon leader in 15th Company, 6th Parachute Regiment with the rank of Oberfeldwebel.

Alexander Uhlig joined IV (Parachute) Battalion, General Göring Regiment on November 2, 1937. He earned his parachutist-rifleman certificate in Stendal. On April 1, 1938 he was sent to 1st Company, 1st Parachute Regiment in Stendal, where he took part in the formation of the regiment.

Uhlig saw action in Poland as an *Obergefreiter*. His first combat drop took place on April 9, 1940, when he and the Schmidt Company were put down near Dombas. Uhlig and his 35 comrades were captured by the Norwegians but were soon freed. He was thus present to help reinforce *General* Dietl's 3rd Mountain Infantry Division at Narvik. On December 1, 1940 he joined the flying personnel of the Luftwaffe and joined 1 Staffel of the Special Purpose Bomber Geschwader, with which he saw action over Crete.

On November 1, 1942 Uhlig became an observer with 2 Staffel, Special Purpose Bomber Geschwader Naples and flew supply missions to Africa. On March 1, 1943 he was promoted to *Oberfeldwebel* and on August 1 of that year received the Iron Cross, First Class.

Uhlig joined the 6th Parachute Regiment under *Oberstleutnant* von der Heydte as it was being formed, and on March 1, 1943 became a platoon leader in the regiment's 8th Company.

On June 5, 1944 the unit was moved to Carentan and during the coming night experienced the dropping of American paratroops. Uhlig took over 16th Company when its commander was killed; he and 35 men eliminated an enemy penetration. They fired on enemy-occupied buildings with Panzerfaust anti-tank weapons and took several hundred prisoners. Uhlig received the Knight's Cross for this action.

On July 31, 1944 Uhlig was taken prisoner by the Americans while withdrawing from the main line of resistance.

KURT VETH

Born on June 1, 1907 in Delmenhorst, Lower Saxony.
Ultimate rank: Major.
Last service position: Commander of II Battalion, 3rd Parachute Regiment.
German Cross in Gold on October 27, 1943.
Wound Badge in Gold on April 10, 1945.
Knight's Cross on September 30, 1944 as commander of II Battalion, 3rd Parachute Regiment with the rank of Hauptmann.
Oak Leaves (not numbered) on April 30, 1945 as commander of I Battalion, 3rd Parachute Regiment (1st Parachute Division) with the rank of Major.

Kurt Veth joined the 63rd Infantry Regiment, Delmenhorst, as a volunteer on April 1, 1935. He was later transferred to the 90th Infantry Regiment in Hamburg-Wentorf, where he was promoted to *Leutnant* on August 1, 1938.

On February 15, 1940 he transferred to the parachute troops and joined the 3rd Parachute Regiment. He was promoted to *Oberleutnant* on November 1, 1940 and on March 31, 1941 was named operations officer of I Battalion, 3rd Parachute Regiment.

Veth and his battalion jumped over Crete and he received the two Iron Crosses on June 10 and 21, 1941.

In the northern sector of the Eastern Front Veth saw action as operations officer of the 3rd Parachute Regiment. He then served a second tour in Russia in 1942-43, on the Kalinin front in Army Group Center's area of operations.

July 15, 1943 found Veth taking part in the German defensive effort in Sicily as company commander of 2nd Company, 3rd Parachute Regiment. Veth repelled a British landing attempt at Agnone. He fought in the front lines at Catenanuova and Centuripe, Aderno and Maletto. Although wounded three times he remained at the front. A fourth wound suffered near Maletto was so serious that he was forced to enter hospital. Veth won the German Cross in Gold during the fighting on Sicily.

Veth returned to his unit for the Third Battle of Cassino. He and his 3rd Company, 3rd Parachute Regiment participated in the attack on Calvary Mountain, which was taken by *Oberfeldwebel* Karl Schmidt in the second assault. Schmidt was awarded the German Cross in Gold. This was Veth's finest hour, and it won him the Knight's Cross. As commander of II Battalion, 3rd Parachute Regiment he fought with unparalleled bravery during the retreat through Italy.

VIKTRO VITALI

Born on April 3, 1920 in Vienna, Austria.
Ultimate rank: Oberleutnant.
Last service position: Commander of 6th Company, 4th Parachute Regiment and leader of a battle group.
Knight's Cross on April 30, 1945 as commander of 5th Company, 4th Parachute Regiment with the rank of Leutnant.

On June 20, 1940 Viktor Vitali joined the 3rd Battery of the 19th Flak Replacement Battalion in Gotha. After various postings to other flak searchlight and flak artillery battalions he was sent on a platoon leaders course. The course, which was held in Vienna, concerned the 2000mm searchlight and various types of remote control equipment.

On April 15, 1944 Vitali, now a *Leutnant,* joined the parachute troops as a volunteer. He began the parachutist-rifleman course in Pont du Mousson in France on April 23, 1944. Vitali joined the 4th Parachute Regiment's II Battalion on May 1, 1944 and became an operations officer in the regimental headquarters. Subsequently he and his regiment were transported to Italy.

From July 20 to September 27, 1944 Vitali fought in the area north of Cassino and at Lake Trasimeno, at Val di Chiana and at the Arno River.

Vitali particularly distinguished himself during the fighting in the Goten Position, where he fought in the Foglia-Metauro River sector. From November 1944 to January 1945 he participated in the German defense of Hill 131 in the Apennines, in the area of Monte Grande. Vitali won the Iron Cross, First Class in the battle for Bologna.

Vitali was a "rock amid the waves" in the battles at the Senio, at Santerno and the Gaina, at Quaderna and Idice, as well as in the bitter fighting to capture the Po crossing. On April 26, 1945 he was promoted to *Oberleutnant* and on the 30th was decorated with the Knight's Cross by *General* Heidrich, commanding general of the I Parachute Corps. Vitali was wounded on May 3 and was taken prisoner by the Americans while in a hospital in Perugia.

HELMUT WAGNER

Born on August 18, 1915 in Köslin, Pomerania.
Ultimate rank: Hauptmann.
Last service position: Commander of 9th Company, 6th Parachute Regiment.
Knight's Cross on January 24, 1942 as a platoon leader in 6th Company, 1st Parachute Regiment with the rank of Leutnant.
Killed in action on June 7, 1944 near St. Côme-du-Mont, Normandy.

Helmut Wagner became a member of the Luftwaffe on April 1, 1938. Exactly a year later he reported to the parachute troops and was assigned to II Battalion, 1st Parachute Regiment, with which he took part in the fighting in Poland. On July 28, 1940 Wagner was awarded the Iron Cross, First Class for his actions in Holland.

During the airborne invasion of Crete Wagner and his platoon from 6th Company, 1st Parachute Regiment came down near Heraklion airfield. Wagner was wounded in the foot even before he landed. In spite of this he fought with great bravery. Wagner was wounded no less than five times in this dramatic struggle for the Greek island. Together with a handful of soldiers he put out of action three English anti-aircraft positions. Wagner personally knocked out one of the few British tanks with hand grenades.

At the urging of *Reichsmarschall* Göring, who had received the 1st Parachute Regiment's account of the battle and read of Wagner's terrific effort, on January 24, 1942 Wagner was decorated with the Knight's Cross.

After recovering from his wounds, in early 1944 Wagner joined the newly-formed 6th Parachute Regiment. He led the regiment's 9th Company and on September 27 was promoted to *Hauptmann.*

Wagner wasn't one to make much of himself, preferring instead to let his actions speak for him. On the second day of the invasion he was killed in the Carentan area by a direct hit by an artillery shell on his dugout.

ERICH WALTHER

**Born on August 5, 1903 in Girden bei Falkenberg, Cottbus District.
Ultimate rank: Generalmajor.
Last service position: Commander of the 2nd Hermann Göring Parachute Panzer-Grenadier Division.
Knight's Cross on May 24, 1940 as commander of I Battalion, 1st Parachute Regiment with the rank of Hauptmann.
German Cross in Gold on April 13, 1942.
Oak Leaves (411th recipient) as commander of the 4th Parachute Regiment with the rank of Oberst.
Swords (131st recipient) as commander of the 2nd Hermann Göring Parachute Panzer-Grenadier Division with the rank of Oberst.
Died on December 26, 1947 in Weimar.**

Erich Walther joined the Berlin Police on April 1, 1924 as a police cadet. In 1933 he transferred to the Wecke State Police Group as a *Leutnant* and on October 1, 1935 became commander of 3rd Company, General Göring Regiment. In May of that year he completed the parachute course and was subsequently promoted to *Hauptmann.* In the war in the west Walther and his I Battalion, 1st Parachute Regiment parachuted into Holland near Dordrecht.

From May 27, 1940 Walther fought in Norway in support of the 3rd Mountain Infantry Division. *General* Dietl personally thanked Walther for his decisive contribution to victory in Norway. On June 19, 1940 he was promoted to *Major.*

On Crete Walther fought alongside III Battalion, 1st Parachute Regiment (Schulz) in the Heraklion area and on May 29 marched into the city at the head of the paratroops.

Walther saw action in Russia in the defensive battle near Leningrad and was awarded the German Cross in Gold for his actions there. On April 20, 1942 Walther was promoted to *Oberst* and in September was appointed commanding officer of the 4th Parachute Regiment.

On the island of Sicily Walther and his troops fought in a defensive role at and north of the Simeto Bridge. At Cassino his regiment defended the much fought over hills.

Walther saw action in the west as commander of the Divisional Battle Group Walther. At Nimwegen and Arnheim he stopped the enemy paratroops. Walther subsequently assumed command of the Hermann Göring 2nd Parachute Panzer-Grenadier Division in East Prussia, with which he faced the Russian onslaught. Promoted to *Generalmajor* on January 30, 1945, on May 8 he was taken prisoner by the Soviets. He was tossed into the camp at Buchenwald where he died a wretched death.

FRIEDRICH-WILHELM WANGERIN

Born on January 27, 1915 in Berlin.
Ultimate rank: Hauptmann.
Last service position: Commander of III Battalion, 16th Parachute Regiment-East.
German Cross in Gold on January 28, 1944.
Knight's Cross on October 24, 1944 as commander of III Battalion, 16th Parachute Regiment-East with the rank of Hauptmann.

Friedrich-Wilhelm Wangerin joined I Battalion of the 67th Infantry Regiment in Berlin-Spandau on October 7, 1935. On December 3, 1939 he was sent to the 477th Infantry Replacement Battalion in Meseritz and there joined the parachute troops. He took the required parachutist-rifleman course from April 1 to June 30, 1940.

Wangerin was promoted to *Leutnant* on January 1, 1940 and served in various adjutant positions. On July 27, 1942 he was named platoon leader in 10th Company, 5th Parachute Regiment.

From November 20, 1942 Wangerin and his regiment saw action in Northwest Africa following the allied landings there. He served with distinction in Tunisia, won both Iron Crosses and was made company commander of 5th Company, 5th Parachute Regiment.

November 1943 found Wangerin and the 5th Parachute Regiment in action in the Ukraine, where they remained until February 1944. On several occasions Wangerin was in the thick of the action, and he was awarded the German Cross in Gold on January 20, 1944.

Wangerin subsequently served as director of training in the Schirmer Battalion and from June 1, 1944 commanded III Battalion of the 16th Parachute Regiment-East (Schirmer).

On October 24 Wangerin received the Honor Roll Clasp for his defensive battle at Kauen and was decorated with the Knight's Cross. After being wounded again he received the Wound Badge in Gold.

After leaving hospital in Jüterbog Wangerin returned to action with the Hermann Göring Parachute Anti-tank Brigade in the Berlin area.

HANS-JOACHIM WECK

Born on December 22, 1920 in Königsberg, East Prussia.
Ultimate rank: Oberleutnant.
Last service position: Commander of 3rd Company, 4th Parachute Regiment in Italy.
Knight's Cross on April 30, 1945 as commander of 3rd Company, 4th Parachute Regiment with the rank of Oberleutnant.

Weck joined the Wehrmacht on July 15, 1940. His first unit was the Königsberg Flight Training Regiment, where he served in the student company. Weck was subsequently sent to flying training school A/B 120 in Jena-Rödingen. On September 1, 1941 he was placed in a wartime officer candidate course and from January 27, 1942 participated in a parachute weapons course in Weissewarthe-Tangerhütte.

On February 19, 1942 Weck joined the 16th Company of the 1st Parachute Replacement Regiment in Stendal. He was promoted to *Oberjäger* on January 1, 1942.

After completing the parachutist-rifleman course at Stendal he was assigned to the Luftwaffe Officer Candidate School at Berlin-Gatow. On December 20, 1942 Weck became a platoon leader in 2nd Company, 4th Parachute Regiment, with which he fought in the winter campaign of 1942-43 in Russia. On March 30, 1943 Wecke returned from Russia.

The Battle of Sicily saw him in action as a *Feldwebel* with his old regiment under *Oberstleutnant* Walther. Weck also fought on the Italian mainland, often at critical points. On January 1, 1944 he was promoted to *Leutnant.*

Weck was named operations officer of I Battalion, 4th Parachute Regiment on June 15, 1944. Later, as the battalion adjutant, he undertook a series of risky reconnaissance and offensive patrols, which on September 29, 1944 won him the Iron Cross, First Class. On October 1 he was placed in charge of 3rd Company, 4th Parachute Regiment and was wounded in an enemy attack on January 22, 1945. Weck returned to action on February 3, 1945 and became company commander of the "Third." He and his company took part in the fighting withdrawal to Bologna and from there into the Po Plain, foiling several breakthrough attempts by enemy armor. On April 30 *General* Heidrich decorated Weck with the Knight's Cross.

HEINRICH WELSKOP

Born on August 8, 1916 in Duisburg.
Ultimate rank: Oberfeldwebel.
Last service position: Platoon leader in 11th Company, 3rd Parachute Regiment.
Knight's Cross on August 21, 1941 as a platoon leader in 11th Company, 3rd Parachute Regiment with the rank of Oberfeldwebel.

"Heiner" Welskop joined I (Light Infantry) Battalion of the General Göring Regiment on November 1, 1937. On April 1, 1939 he was assigned to 6th Company, 1st Parachute Regiment and on December 1 of that year was promoted to *Oberjäger*.

For acts of bravery during the battle for Fortress Holland Welskop was decorated with the Iron Cross, First and Second Class on May 25 and 26, 1940. On June 1 he was promoted to *Feldwebel*.

On May 1, 1941 Welskop took over a platoon of the 11th Company, 3rd Parachute Regiment and led the unit in action in the airborne invasion of Crete. His battalion commander was *Major* Heilmann. The 11th Company was dropped in middle of the barren mountains south of Privolia and had to fight its way through the enemy to I Battalion.

It initially seemed as if the Welskop platoon had been swallowed up by the earth. The company commander was killed; his body was later found at the side of the road.

Acting on his own initiative Welskop stormed a hill near Chania which protruded into the enemy positions. He and his platoon held this decisive position against fierce counterattacks by the New Zealanders. It was bitter fighting, often at close quarters.

Oberst Heidrich eventually ordered the hill abandoned, but the order did not get through to Welskop. He held the small salient in the front alone against superior enemy forces. This heroic action won him the Knight's Cross.

Welskop saw action with his regiment in the campaign in Russia; he was wounded but remained with his men.

Weiskop also served with his regiment in Italy and repeatedly distinguished himself by steadfastly holding the positions assigned to him. His platoon saw in him a good comrade and true friend.

WALTER WERNER

Born on July 11, 1917 in Brand-Erbisdorf, Freiburg District, Silesia. Ultimate rank: Leutnant.
Last service position: Platoon leader in the 1st Company of the 1st Parachute Pioneer Battalion.
Knight's Cross on June 9, 1944 as squad leader in 1st Company, 1st Parachute Pioneer Battalion with the rank of Feldwebel.

Walter Werner joined the German Armed Forces on November 7, 1938 and from April 16 to June 30, 1939 received basic training as an airframe electrician at Jüterbog Aviation Technical School. Werner also trained as a pioneer and took part in an NCO course. On May 1, 1942 he was promoted to *Oberjäger.*

Werner took part in the campaign in Poland in the rear area of operations, saw action in France and fought in the campaign in the Balkans from April 6 to May 6, 1941.

On November 1, 1942 he was transferred to the 1st Parachute Pioneer Battalion's 1st Company and was to prove himself in subsequent actions with the unit.

Werner received the Iron Cross, Second Class during the second paratroop action in Russia from October 28, 1942 to March 31, 1943.

From July 22, 1943 Werner fought in southern Italy. During the night of March 1, 1944 he and his company moved into Cassino city, where his company was divided among the units of II Battalion, 3rd Parachute Regiment. While the 2nd Platoon was deployed near the penitentiary, *Oberjäger* Werner and 3rd Squad took over the fish market sector. Ground troops attacked following an enemy bombing raid ground; the Neuhoff and Werner strongpoints fought heroically. Werner undertook a number of offensive patrols and drove the enemy from the northern part of the city. *Oberfeldwebel* Neuhoff and *Oberjäger* Werner received the Knight's Cross. Werner was wounded on May 4, 1944 and on August 28 was promoted to *Leutnant.* On May 2, 1945 he and his platoon were taken prisoner by the British.

KARL-HANS WITTIG

Born on July 27, 1918 in Seegläsen, Züllichau District, Brandenburg.
Ultimate rank: Leutnant.
Last service position: Platoon leader in the 11th Company of the 1st
Parachute Regiment.
German Cross in Gold on March 20, 1943.
Knight's Cross on May 2, 1944 as a patrol leader and Feldwebel in the
11th Company of the 1st Parachute Regiment.
Wound Badge in Gold in March 1943 near Orel.
Died on December 29, 1984 in Nuremberg.

Karl-Hans Wittig joined the Wehrmacht on October 1, 1937 and served initially in the General Göring Regiment. From this formation came the units for the 1st Parachute Regiment.

Wittig won the Iron Cross, Second Class as an *Obergefreiter* for the action at Dordrecht, Holland. He received the Iron Cross, First Class for the action at The Hague. Wittig saw action in Crete as an *Oberjäger* with the 11th Company.

Promoted to *Feldwebel*, Wittig's greatest period began in Russia during the winter operations of 1942-43. He led the security platoon of an offensive patrol at Durnewo. When the patrol was cut off Wittig led the way to freedom, bringing 18 prisoners and much captured equipment with him.

During the offensive and defensive actions at Velikye Luki Wittig led the battalion point forces. Unfortunately the German attempt to relieve the surrounded fortress ended failure.

South of Gribushino Wittig led the battalion point forces in a counterattack, took a hill away from the enemy and fought off all attempts to regain it. Here Wittig was wounded for the fourth time; he was awarded the German Cross in Gold.

In the subsequent fighting near Stolbetskoye Wittig destroyed four of eight attacking tanks from close range. He assumed command of the company after the company commander was badly wounded, stormed a hill and secured a gap in the front southeast of Orel. There he was wounded for the fifth time.

Promoted to *Leutnant,* Wittig fought on the Western Front. In late autumn 1944 he was captured near Mons, Belgium.

RUDOLF WITZIG

Born on August 14, 1916 in Röhlinghausen, Westphalia.
Ultimate rank: Major.
Last service position: Commander of the 18th Parachute Regiment.
German Cross in Gold on October 17, 1943.
Knight's Cross on May 10, 1940 as commander of the Airborne Landing Group Gran*it* with the rank of Oberleutnant.
Oak Leaves (662nd recipient) on November 25, 1944 as commander of I Battalion, 21st Parachute Pioneer Regiment with the rank of Major.

On April 1, 1935 Rudolf Witzig joined the 16th Pioneer Battalion in Höxter as an officer candidate. Two years later, on April 20, 1937, he became a *Leutnant* and served as a platoon leader in the 31st Pioneer Battalion, Höxter. From there Witzig reported to the parachute troops as a volunteer on August 1, 1938 and joined the Parachute Infantry Battalion under *Major* Heidrich. A year later, after transferring to the Luftwaffe, he was an *Oberleutnant* and leader of the Koch Parachute Assault Battalion's pioneer platoon.

Witzig's greatest feat was the capture of Eben Emael on May 10, 1940. A special announcement on May 11 lauded the accomplishments of Witzig and his airborne landing group. The day before he had been decorated with the Knight's Cross. On May 16 he received an early promotion to *Hauptmann.*

During the Crete operation Witzig led the 9th Company of the Parachute Assault Regiment. Wounded there, he was transferred from the Luftwaffe hospital in Athens to several other hospitals.

On May 10, 1942 Witzig was placed in command of the Corps Parachute Pioneer Battalion and on August 24 of that year was promoted to *Major.* From November 1942 he and his battalion served in Tunisia under *Oberst* von Manteuffel, *General* von Broich and *General* Bülowius and were incorporated into the Barenthin Luftwaffe Regiment. The defensive successes in the northern sector of the Tunisian Front are closely linked with his name.

Witzig became commanding officer of I Battalion, 21st Parachute Pioneer Battalion on June 15, 1944 and at the same time was placed in charge of the regiment. Witzig and his unit were mentioned in the supplement to the Wehrmacht communique of August 8, 1944 after destroying 27 enemy tanks near Kumele.

On December 16, 1944 he became commanding officer of the 18th Parachute Regiment, with which he went into captivity on May 8, 1945. On May 7 he was placed on the Honor Roll of the Luftwaffe.

HILMAR ZAHN

Born on September 6, 1919 in Wiesbaden-Rambach.
Ultimate rank: Hauptmann.
Last service position: Commander of 5th Company, 1st Parachute Regiment.
Wound Badge in Gold on June 3, 1944.
Knight's Cross on June 9, 1944 as commander of 5th Company, 1st Parachute Regiment with the rank of Oberleutnant.

Hilmar Zahn joined the 5th Infantry Regiment's 5th Company in Bad Kreuznach on November 2, 1937. He was transferred to the Luftwaffe on April 1, 1938 and was assigned to the air base at Mannheim-Sandhofen. From there he joined JG 133 in Mannheim on March 18, 1939. On October 1 of that year Zahn was promoted to *Obergefreiter* and on January 19, 1940 signed up for a twelve-year period of service. He initially served in the 28th Luftwaffe Construction Company, on February 1, 1940 was promoted to *Unteroffizier* and completed two wartime officer preparation courses. Zahn passed a platoon leaders course at the Luftwaffe battle school in Gross Born-Linde in Pomerania. On April 20, 1942 he was promoted to *Leutnant*.

Zahn took the parachutist-rifleman course in Wittstock. On June 3, 1942 he joined the 1st Parachute Regiment as a platoon leader in the 5th Company. Zahn went to Russia with this unit in the winter of 1942-43. He saw action at the front's hot spots and was wounded during a patrol toward Alexeyevka.

In the Italian Theater Zahn, an *Oberleutnant* since July 14, 1943, led the 1st Parachute Regiment's 5th Company in the battles in the Ortona area and finally at Cassino. There he was one of the bravest of the defenders, leading offensive and reconnaissance patrols and undertaking counterattacks and raids. Zahn's actions won him the Knight's Cross.

On March 2, 1944 Zahn was wounded badly. His right leg had to be amputated above the knee. Nevertheless he returned to the field forces. Zahn was promoted to *Hauptmann* for bravery in the face of the enemy and fought in the defensive struggle in Italy until May 2, 1945. He was released from allied captivity in Steinbach am Brenner on June 30, 1945.

OTTO ZIERACH

Born on January 26, 1907 in Eberswalde near Berlin.
Ultimate rank: Major.
Last service position: Officer in the staff of the II Parachute Corps.
Knight's Cross on May 15, 1940 as Ia of the Koch Parachute Assault Battalion.
Died on August 12, 1976 in Nachrodt-Versede, Märkisch District.

Otto Zierach entered the Brandenburg-Havel Police School on April 13, 1928 and from there joined the Wecke Special Purpose Police Battalion as a Police *Oberwachtmeister.* Zierach became a member of the General Göring Regiment when the police battalion was so renamed. On April 1, 1938 *Oberfeldwebel* Zierach was taken on strength by 1st Company, 1st Parachute Regiment. He was promoted to *Hauptfeldwebel* the same day.

On February 16, 1940, immediately after the formation of the Koch Parachute Assault Battalion, Zierach became the unit's Ia. *Hauptmann* Walter Koch, who was placed in command of the airborne operations against the fortress of Eben Emael and the four bridges over the Albert Canal, found Zierach a capable and knowledgeable assistant.

The battalion staff jumped with Assault Group Beton near Vroenhoven Bridge. The defenders were prevented from destroying the bridge. For this action and his work in preparing all the others, Zierach was awarded the Knight's Cross and on May 20, 1940 received an early promotion to *Hauptmann.*

Zierach took part in the action on Crete as special duties officer; on February 26, 1942 he joined the staff of the Luftwaffe Division Meindl. For a time he led the 1st Luftwaffe Division's III Battalion. Zierach subsequently joined the staff of II Parachute Corps and on January 8, 1944 was sent by *General* Meindl, the corps' commanding general, to the Luftwaffe Air Warfare Academy in Berlin-Gatow.

In Normandy Zierach saw action to the bitter end on the Ems River, serving as a staff officer with II Parachute Corps. On May 8, 1945 he was made a prisoner of war by the British but was soon released.